"Whether your passion is mountaineering or business, *Lead Like a Guide* makes a compelling case that the ultimate act of leadership is helping others reach as high as they can."

—**Adam Grant, Wharton professor and**
New York Times–**best-selling author of**
Give and Take **and** *Originals*

"An accomplished leadership educator, Chris Maxwell is as comfortable on a mountain peak as he is in a classroom. In his book he brings together his amazing talents and provides the reader clear lessons and insights on some of the most valuable leadership principles, which are as applicable to the board room or government as they are to being part of a mountain-climbing team."

—**Jeffrey D. McCausland, PhD, former dean, U.S. Army**
War College; national security consultant for CBS Radio
and TV; and founder and CEO, Diamond6 Leadership
and Strategy, LLC

"By looking far afield we sometimes see best what is most vital for home. From interviews with mountain guides and those they have led, Chris Maxwell offers absorbing accounts in *Lead Like a Guide* that show that thinking strategically, appraising risk, and empowering followers are essential not only for mountaineering but also for management."

—**Michael Useem, PhD, professor and director of the**
Leadership Center, Wharton School, University of
Pennsylvania, and co-author of *Boards That Lead*

"Chris Maxwell succinctly uncovers the true spirit of leadership by exploring the way guides adapt and improvise, under often adverse and dangerous conditions, to best serve the safety of the experience and the growth of the individual—natural and servant leadership exposed."

—**Andrew Muir (Dr.), CEO, Wilderness Foundation**
Global and Wilderness Foundation Africa

"A book full of powerful insights from both guides and participants, with valuable lessons about leadership."

—**Monica L. Pugh, director,**
Center for Student Leadership, University of Monterrey,
Monterrey, Mexico

"As an executive coach and leadership consultant, just about everything in my work is filtered through my lens of over 30 years spent in the business of guiding others in the wilderness. Chris Maxwell has thoroughly researched, and eloquently captured, the leadership lessons of others as well as his own, through his extensive experience in the mountains. *Lead Like a Guide* will inspire and engage the reader to be a better leader, whether with peers or in the boardroom."
                    —**John Kanengieter, director for leadership, National
                    Outdoor Leadership School; principal, Kanengieter
                    Consulting Group; and former mountain guide**

"At last! In true adventurous style, Chris Maxwell has dared to go where others have not and puts tangible value on the hidden-in-the-shadows and intensely relevant skills that professional guides use every day. He offers a razor-sharp view through a rarely seen window to explain the tools guides use to help people from all walks of life achieve extraordinary goals in challenging and uncertain circumstances. *Lead Like a Guide* offers a well-researched master class for anyone to learn these robust real-time principles, but without the risks (and smelly clothes!)."
                    —**Graham Charles, polar expedition leader
                    and outdoor educator**

"The six strengths of a mountain guide identified by Chris Maxwell are useful for any leader or manager of an entrepreneurial enterprise if it is to thrive in conditions of uncertainty. Anyone who seeks to lead a team, however large or small, can learn from and benefit from applying these strengths to their own way of working."
                    —**Nunzio Quacquarelli, managing director,
                    Quacquarelli Symonds Limited (UK)**

Lead Like a Guide

Lead Like a Guide

How World-Class Mountain Guides Inspire Us to Be Better Leaders

Christopher I. Maxwell, PhD

Foreword by Rodrigo Jordan, PhD,
Mount Everest and K2 Expedition Leader

 PRAEGER™

An Imprint of ABC-CLIO, LLC
Santa Barbara, California • Denver, Colorado

Library of Congress Cataloging-in-Publication Data

Names: Maxwell, Christopher I., author.
Title: Lead like a guide : how world-class mountain guides inspire us to be better leaders / Christopher I. Maxwell, PhD ; foreword by Rodrigo Jordan, PhD, Mount Everest and K2 Expedition Leader.
Description: Santa Barbara, California : Praeger, [2016] | Includes bibliographical references and index. | Description based on print version record and CIP data provided by publisher; resource not viewed.
Identifiers: LCCN 2016033075 (print) | LCCN 2016020711 (ebook) | ISBN 9781440844171 (E-book) | ISBN 9781440844164 (hard copy : alk. paper)
Subjects: LCSH: Leadership. | Mountaineering guides (Persons)
Classification: LCC HD57.7 (print) | LCC HD57.7 .M39357 2016 (ebook) | DDC 658.4/092—dc23
LC record available at https://lccn.loc.gov/2016033075

ISBN: 978-1-4408-4416-4
EISBN: 978-1-4408-4417-1

20 19 18 17 16   1 2 3 4 5

This book is also available as an eBook.

Praeger
An Imprint of ABC-CLIO, LLC

ABC-CLIO, LLC
130 Cremona Drive, P.O. Box 1911
Santa Barbara, California 93116-1911
www.abc-clio.com

This book is printed on acid-free paper (∞)

Manufactured in the United States of America

The guide is more than a mere machine for climbing rocks and ice slopes, for knowing the weather and the way. He does not climb for himself, he throws open the gates of his mountains as a gardener opens the gates of his garden.
—GASTON RÉBUFFAT (*Starlight and Storm*)

Life is change. How it differs from the rocks.
—PAUL KANTNER (Lyric from *Crown of Creation*)

Contents

Foreword

The sun had already begun to hide behind the majestic mountains. Through the window of the bus I could enjoy the magnificent rock spires, now painted in fiery red, that surround Baños Morales, the Mecca of Central Andes mountaineering. My face stuck to the glass looking voraciously at those spectacular summits, as if I were a small boy standing outside the window of the local chocolate store.

I couldn't hold together all my thoughts and emotions, as my very first climbing trip to the Andes was about to start. Excitement devoured me: tomorrow morning I would be off to the high summits.

I felt lucky: my guide was strong and knowledgeable. Not too young—he had significant experience—but not too old. I wanted to go as fast as I could. I wanted to climb the highest number of summits I could in the short week ahead.

The following day we had a very efficient and safe climb. The guide was always in front of me, moving quickly and showing the way. He was in great shape and it took almost all my energy just to keep up with him. We were able to nail two beautiful peaks in that one day, and I was filled with satisfaction.

It seemed that the guide was happy with his client, as he encouraged me to attempt other summits on the following days. I did, and we certainly had a succession of great ascents.

Nevertheless, two days before my week was over, a strange sensation invaded me. I felt there was something missing. We had succeeded in climbing many peaks, but I was not elated by this success. Had I enjoyed the climbs thoroughly? I wasn't sure.

Over a glass of beer my guide heard my concerns with great affection and respect. "Tomorrow you will climb with Claudio, the oldest guide among us. I will introduce you to him."

By early morning the following day, we were at the foot of a beautiful rock spire. We had already tied ourselves in to the rope and I was waiting for Claudio to start climbing, but nothing happened. After what seemed to be quite a long time, he simply said, "Go!" and waved his hand for me to start climbing. At first I did not understand, so he repeated, "Go! Go!" He wanted me to be in front.

I led the first pitch and belayed him while he climbed. Slowly, but graciously and with seemingly no effort, he joined me and repeated again, "Go! Go!" Nothing else. "Go!"

I was on fire. I was now ahead. I was making the calls, I was taking the risks, I was making mistakes. I was really climbing.

When we reached the summit I had this profound feeling that I had done it, that I had not been pulled up the climb. I had genuinely climbed the mountain.

Claudio had made the ultimate guiding action: he had empowered me to grow, to expand my capacities, to go by myself.

It is one of my most cherished moments, and one of the most important lessons I have learned in my long climbing career: *Good mountain guides empower.*

This is why I was so deeply moved when I read that that is one of the crucial leadership strengths of guides that Chris Maxwell extracts from his magnificent intellectual exploration on what leaders in the most diverse fields of action can learn from mountain guides. As good mountain guides do, leaders empower others to "climb their own summits."

I was even more thrilled to read about the other five leadership strengths Chris unearthed from the mountain guiding world, and presents in this book. I now cherish them all and repeatedly go back and apply them, not only when guiding but, above all, in my entrepreneurial and social work to alleviate poverty in South America.

Chris's chapter, "Guides Facilitate the Development of Trust," is one of many examples that I have seen work in fields other than mountain guiding. In a great number of poverty alleviation initiatives in Chile, there was a group of very well intentioned "outsiders" who wanted to help a poverty-stricken community of "insiders." All of those initiatives—where trust was not built between these two groups—failed. Thus, in Fundación Vertical's social programs, we have incorporated a long series of trust-building activities before, during, and after the execution of these initiatives. Even though this makes the initiatives much longer to complete, it is the only way to expect any long-term success, because it ensures the establishment of the required vital confidence between outsiders and insiders.

Chris valuably includes a number of lessons learned and applied, which present excellent examples of his students' experiences when they applied these six leadership strengths in their own work environments. This strongly validates that the way mountain guides exercise leadership can indeed be transferred to other realities, from the factory floor to the boardroom.

The interviews with the guides add to the text that which is so many times absent from academic works: the human dimension of it all. These fascinating and entertaining interviews provide from the very beginning a unique emotional setting that lasts throughout the entire book.

The valuable lessons Chris distills from mountain guides could not have been obtained without his very powerful combination of academic research and hard work in the field. It is in the initial interviews and the overall moving writing of

Rodrigo Jordan led the first South American team to reach the summit of Mount Everest and has led successful expeditions to some of the world's highest peaks, including K2 and Lhotse. He is chairman of Vertical, S.A., an organization focused on experiential leadership education, based in Santiago, Chile. Rodrigo serves on the advisory board of the Anne and John McNulty Leadership Program at the Wharton School of the University of Pennsylvania. He holds a PhD in innovation from Oxford University. (Photo courtesy of Rodrigo Jordan)

Lead Like a Guide that one senses Chris's very deep care—I'd rather say love—for two critical components of human growth and development: natural wild places and the unique education that can take place in them.

Ulrich Inderbinen, the world's oldest mountain guide, died on June 14, 2004, at age 103. *The Economist* compared Mr. Inderbinen to early Everest climber George Leigh Mallory, who famously said he wanted to climb Everest "because it is there."

> Mallory crystallized a romantic vision of the mountaineer, chasing after dreams on ice-wrapped summits far from home and hearth. Ulrich Inderbinen could not have been more different. He went up mountains not because they were there, but because he was. He died gently, in his bed. And though he may not have been the first to climb the Matterhorn, he seems to have climbed it best.

I strongly believe that Chris Maxwell's *Lead Like a Guide* will help you lead and live at your best.

Rodrigo Jordan, PhD

Preface

Princeton, New Jersey: In a packed corporate auditorium, a gathering of financial executives listened closely as blind mountaineer Erik Weihenmayer recounted what he had learned from his successful bid to climb the highest mountain on each continent, a group known as the "Seven Summits." Weihenmayer told his rapt audience that a firm can harness the energy of overcoming uncertainty and hardship in much the same manner as mountaineers—linked together as climbers are roped together on a mountain, inspired by a common vision, following a common purpose, and working interdependently to face and overcome adversity. "Adversity," he told the audience, "is not the obstacle, but the pathway."[1]

Jackson Hole, Wyoming: In a hand-hewn log cabin nestled at the base of Wyoming's imposing Grand Teton, veteran guide Jack Turner addressed a small group of business students. In modern life, he told them, a variety of experts, such as financial advisors, are there to help shield individuals from many common risks. "But in the wilderness," he said, "we tend to leave those experts behind, and you have to make those decisions. In climbing, you must learn to trust, not in experts, but in your own abilities and the abilities of your partners. Climbing is a good way to learn about yourself, and whether you will meet or turn away from risk. And that's a function of your trust environment."[2]

Philadelphia, Pennsylvania: During a University of Pennsylvania executive education session, Eugenio "Kiko" Guzman, a high-altitude mountaineer and guide based in Santiago, Chile, sets the scene: His team is making a summit attempt on Lhotse, the world's fourth-highest peak. Guzman's team has spotted something falling from high on the Lhotse face, above Camp 4. They radio the information to the advance team, which is climbing from Camp 2 to Camp 3. Both teams attempt to identify what fell, but it is late in the day and the visibility is now poor. No other calls come over the radio. The following day, as the advance group moves up slowly behind a long line of Everest climbers, the object finally becomes clear—it's a climber who has fallen from the Lhotse face and has lain exposed to the elements overnight at over 7,000 meters. As they approach the fallen climber, now in a coma and near death, they detect some movement. Already high in the death zone themselves, what should the teams do?[3]

More than a few lessons relevant to organizational leadership can be drawn from both triumph and tragedy in the mountains. To me, this explains why mountaineers and world-class guides are so often asked by company leaders to talk about how the challenges they have confronted during their expeditions relate to those of organizations facing their own rapidly changing landscapes. As mountaineer and educator Edwin Bernbaum writes, "Just as Everest stretches people to do more than they thought they could, so companies want to stretch their employees to help the organization reach the loftiest goals, to be number one in the field, to provide the best product or service in the industry group."[4]

A distant mountain peak beckoning through the clouds effectively serves as a metaphor for an organization's vision and top-level goals. Visualizing standing on the summit, with its promise of uncharted horizons beyond, stirs the heart and inspires people to reach as high as they can. Inspiration alone, however, will not produce sustained or tangible change in an enterprise.[5] With a clear vision, a sense of purpose, a committed team, and a path to the summit identified, what happens next in both mountaineering and in organizations is largely dependent on leadership. As Michael Useem, a management professor and director of the Center for Leadership and Change Management at the Wharton School of the University of Pennsylvania, writes, "Leadership requires strategic thinking, decisive action, personal integrity, and other worthy qualities." Yet, he adds, "Converting such abstract qualities into practice is often an elusive process. Indeed, few behavioral concepts defy translation into reality as much as those that involve leadership."[6]

In a bold move to resolve this dilemma, Useem and his team created Wharton Leadership Ventures, a program designed to offer business students hands-on leadership development opportunities ranging from brief workshops to longer, physically demanding expeditions.[7] *Lead Like a Guide* focuses on the innovative partnership of educators, world-class mountain guides, and participants who—by engaging in brief expeditions in wild places—experience, reflect on, and draw meaningful leadership lessons from their own actions and those of their fellow travelers. Rigorous enough to be a true stretch experience, the expeditions require advance reading and a commitment on the part of the participant to engage in a process of self-discovery and character and leadership development. From the foot of Mount Everest to the Rockies, from Patagonia to Antarctica, from New Zealand to Iceland and far beyond, in a little more than 10 years this novel effort has introduced more than 3,000 business students at Wharton to the value of learning from experience while confronting ambiguous and uncertain environments and tasks, solving new problems, and working with and leading expedition teams.

As an early participant in and, later, a contributor to this effort, I soon became particularly intrigued with the capacity of expert guides to both model and teach leadership. In *Lead Like a Guide* I describe my 10-year research project to discover the leadership strengths of mountain guides; to learn how these same strengths help their clients reach as high, and often higher, than they ever thought possible; and to create a leadership framework that readers can apply in their own lives.

In the process of writing this book, I traveled on a guided expedition to the foot of Mount Everest with a group of mid-career executives; organized and traveled with over 200 undergraduate business students on 21 expeditions in the United States, Quebec, Mexico, Peru, Patagonia, and Iceland; and trekked with a group of MBAs on a remote Patagonian island located on the southern shore of the Beagle Channel, just to the south of Tierra del Fuego. Both on and off the trail, I learned a great deal from my interviews, discussions, and experiences with a number of guide organizations.

Exum Mountain Guides is North America's oldest mountain guide service, based since 1929 in Grand Teton National Park in Wyoming. Kevin Fedarko, a writer for *Outside* magazine, calls the Exum guide service the "crowning ambition of working guides all across America."[8] In 2005, Al Read, then president of Exum, opened the way for me to interview 11 of Exum's most experienced guides, and these interviews helped me begin to identify the leadership strengths of world-class guides that I describe in this book. Five climbs of the Grand Teton with Exum guides, and several more climbs of other Teton Range peaks, gave me a first-hand look at how these guides apply these strengths in practice. I also observed a preseason training session in the Tetons for incoming Exum guides, and attended a number of Exum guide presentations at the Grand Teton Climbers' Ranch and at an Exum Guides' Day preseason meeting and educational session.

Vertical, S.A., a guide organization based in Santiago, Chile, was founded in 1993 by mountaineer and educator Rodrigo Jordan, PhD. Focused on experiential leadership education, Vertical conducts international expeditions; provides human capital consulting; operates a professional institute, Instituto Vertical, dedicated to training young people to enter the eco-tourism field; and runs a nonprofit foundation, Fundación Vertical. While in Santiago I interviewed six Vertical expedition guides and the directors of both the professional institute and the foundation, attended a Vertical leadership development session for executives of a company headquartered in Santiago, observed an experiential training session in the mountains for University of Chile business students, and traveled with several of the Vertical guides on an expedition.

I also learned a great deal from a number of other key guide partners in the United States and abroad, including traveling with *Aerial Boundaries Mountain Guides* on nine expeditions in Wyoming, Utah, Peru, and Patagonia and *Icelandic Mountain Guides* on four expeditions on glaciers and snow peaks in Iceland. Additional details on these guides and their organizations are included in Chapters 1 and 2, and also in the appendix.

THE SIX LEADERSHIP STRENGTHS OF WORLD-CLASS MOUNTAIN GUIDES

Expert mountain guides demonstrate a number of complementary leadership strengths that influence those they travel with in meaningful and lasting ways. While a guide's summit-bound clients may learn a variety of technical skills during their climb, guides also expose clients to a masterful array of leadership strengths, which can drive home some life-changing lessons long after the adventure is over.

First, a guide rapidly establishes positive interactions with clients, which draws on emotional and social intelligence. Second, a guide accurately senses when conditions call for a change in leadership style, and makes that change smoothly. Third, a guide identifies and builds on a client's strengths, and provides a supportive space for growth and development. Fourth, a guide creates an environment of trust, imparting confidence in their own skills as a guide while also helping clients learn to trust themselves and their teammates. Fifth, a guide attends to the welfare of clients as weather or mountain conditions change, accurately assessing and managing risk in an environment of uncertainty. Finally, rather than holding a singular focus on the summit, a guide retains the ability to see the big picture throughout the adventure.

Each leadership strength detailed in the following chapters includes supporting research from the fields of management, leadership, and positive psychology. Many chapters also include direct quotes from the guides whom I interviewed, as well as selections from written reflections by those who have participated in the climbs and treks that I organized. An *In Practice* section (how this leadership strength applied to a participant who is now in the workplace) and a checklist of *Action Steps* to help build skills are included towards the end of Chapters 5 through 10.

- Chapter 1 takes you on a trek to the foot of Mount Everest, and explains why a top business school developed a leadership development program that includes expeditions to remote and wild places.

- Chapter 2 introduces you to Vertical, an innovative South American guiding organization that specializes in educational expeditions. You will meet Rodrigo Jordan, the founder of Vertical, and some of Vertical's top guides, whose mountaineering expeditions include K2, Everest, Lhotse, and more.

- In Chapter 3 we visit Exum Mountain Guides, a legendary mountain guide service based in Grand Teton National Park, Wyoming. The spectacular Teton Range peaks rise almost vertically from the Jackson Hole valley, and offer some of the finest climbing routes in North America. From the founding of Exum in the 1920s to the present day, its guides have built and maintained a reputation for excellence in guiding.

- Chapter 4 takes a close look at Christian Santelices, a guide with whom I have traveled for more than 10 years. From his early days as a young climber who spent 19 days clipped to a sheer rock face in Patagonia, to his current status as an

Figure P-1   The six leadership strengths of world-class mountain guides.

internationally certified mountain guide, I draw key lessons about leading in challenging environments that we will revisit in the subsequent chapters.

- Chapter 5 introduces readers to the first leadership strength of world-class mountain guides: social intelligence. Guides learn quickly that building and maintaining positive relationships in tough conditions demands sensitivity and the ability to put others at ease. Expedition participant Christian Hoogerheyde, a product manager at Socrata, a cloud software company, tells what he observed in his guide and how it applied to his work as a business consultant.

- In Chapter 6, the topic is the guide's ability to adopt a flexible leadership style to match the skill level of clients and changing conditions on the mountain. One guide uses *teach, coach, guide* as an illustration of how different leadership styles are helpful when guiding clients in the backcountry. Expedition participant Seychelle Hicks, a customer success manager lead at BloomReach, a Silicon Valley big-data digital-marketing startup, tells how her guide's use of different leadership styles on the trail influenced her own practice at work.

- Chapter 7 discusses the importance of empowerment. One of the key leadership strengths of guides is the ability to identify and build on a client's strengths, and to provide the space for growth and development, even under challenging conditions. Expedition participant Edmund Reese, an executive at American Express, explains the benefits of his efforts to empower his staff in the workplace.

- Chapter 8 introduces the concept of trust. Guides know that trust is critical for climbers who are bonded together by a rope. We will learn how faith and confidence are related to trust, and how guides help clients build trust in themselves and in their teammates. Expedition participant John Sims tells how what he learned from his guides about trust has helped him as an executive at Snowden Lane Partners, a financial services firm.

- In Chapter 9 we examine the meaning of risk in challenging environments. Guides know that in a modern world that shelters many of us from risk, outdoor activities present the challenges as well as the opportunities of uncertainty. How guides manage risk and leverage uncertainty is the result of long experience and measured judgment. Expedition participant Lyndsey Bunting, a senior financial analyst at Birchbox, explains how an appreciation for risk and uncertainty applied to her prior service in the Peace Corps, and applies to her current work in business.

- Chapter 10 brings home the meaning of looking at the big picture. It is understandable that an expedition participant may be focused on reaching the summit, but wise guides advise that a more holistic view is safer and can be more meaningful. Expedition participant Deborah Horn, a category manager at Microsoft, tells how her search for a fulfilling position was influenced by an appreciation for the journey.

- Chapter 11 brings the book to a close by illustrating how expedition participant Sarah Skye Gilbert, now a program officer at the Bill and Melinda Gates Foundation, has found applications for several of the leadership strengths of guides in her work in global health.

Why should *you* lead like a guide? When you do so, your influence can have a positive impact well beyond your own immediate network. Nicholas Christakis, MD, PhD, a Harvard professor who is both a physician and a social scientist, and James Fowler, PhD, a professor and social scientist at the University of California, San Diego, describe how a wide variety of emotions and behaviors can spread within social networks.[9,10] In their book, *Connected,* they write,

> Together, as we began to think about the idea that people are connected in vast social networks, we realized that social influence does not end with the people we know. If we affect our friends, and they affect their friends, then our actions can potentially affect people we have never met.[11]

Now consider what can happen in your own network as you begin to lead like a guide—showing sensitivity toward others, being thoughtful about the impact of *how* you lead, building others up, developing trusting relationships, accurately assessing and managing risk, and maintaining a holistic view as you reach for your own summits.
Lead Like a Guide!

Acknowledgments

The lessons I have learned along the way are many, and I'm grateful to all of the guides and the many participants who have taken part in this learning experience over the past decade. I'm especially grateful for the assistance many former Wharton School program participants provided as this work was being completed. The members of the Wharton Leadership Ventures Undergraduate Advisory Board, and the many venture coordinators, can take much of the credit for making the expeditions that I describe happen. Lyndsey Bunting helped me a great deal with research in the early stages of the project, and was a key participant on the first two Grand Teton mountaineering ventures. Others who provided research assistance and work-related reflections include Richard Hillen, William Arbuckle, Jacqueline Stein, Seychelle Hicks, Yang Sun, Xenia Kolesnikov, Mansi Jain, Joo Yeon Kim, Courtney Gardner, Vikram Madan, Edmund Reese, John Sims, Deborah Horn, Christian Hoogerheyde, Triston Francis, James Calderwood, Sarah Skye Gilbert, and Evan Rosenbaum. Evan, who participated in treks in Utah, Iceland, and Peru, helped me create the illustrations in the book, provided input on content, and assisted with my website, www.leadlikeaguide.com. Many, many other participants shared the good times and the tough times of the expeditions with me, and generously shared their reflections. To all of these, I owe a great debt of thanks.

Special thanks are due to Al Read of Exum Mountain Guides, who helped greatly by encouraging his team of world-class guides to meet with me early in the process, and to Rodrigo Jordan, PhD, who so kindly allowed me to meet with the Vertical staff in Santiago, Chile. Professor Mike Useem provided early encouragement and support for this project through the Wharton Center for Leadership and Change Management. My longtime friend and colleague, Dr. Anne Greenhalgh, deputy director of the McNulty Leadership Program at Wharton, was especially helpful in supporting the establishment and funding of the undergraduate ventures program.

Jeff Klein, executive director of the McNulty Leadership Program, read and made thoughtful comments on an early draft of the manuscript. Several vice deans of the Wharton undergraduate division, especially Professor Georgette Phillips and Dr. Barbara Kahn, bravely allowed me to persist with organizing and running expeditions in wild and remote places despite their fears that I might lose or drop a student or two along the way. I brought them all back.

Thanks also go to Wharton staff members Meredith Stone, Lindy Black-Margida, Kate FitzGerald, and Sarah Merusi Danyau, who joined me and helped support teams on the Utah, Wyoming, Peru, and Iceland expeditions. The staff of the Leadership Center at the University of Monterrey, Mexico, including Dr. Alicia Canton, Monica Pugh, Alma Ramirez, Monica Bilbao, and Juan Carlos Eschevarria welcomed us to Mexico and provided some extraordinary outdoor experiences. I am also very grateful to Vertical and its guides Gabriel Becker, Willie Parra, Fernando Yañez, and Nicolas Danyau, for allowing me to travel with them on a Wharton MBA leadership expedition to Isla Navarino, a truly remote and beautiful island at the southernmost tip of Chilean Patagonia. Sarah and Nico Danyau kindly allowed me to share their tent—and cooked some amazing meals, too. Canned tuna with spaghetti sauce can taste pretty good in the wild . . .

My longtime friend and guide Christian Santelices, who has guided my teams and me on spectacular expeditions in three countries, is one of the most knowledgeable and considerate people I know. His leadership on the trail and in the mountains has inspired me and countless participants on their own leadership journeys. I especially treasure the occasional reconnaissance trips Christian and I have taken as, in a relaxed mood and without a team of participants to care for, we explored new ground and set up subsequent ventures. One very memorable reconnaissance trip in Peru had Christian, Peruvian guide Marco Palomino, Kathy, and me smiling—laughing out loud, really—from beginning to end. Christian and his wife Sue guided us on our first venture to Patagonia, and we have often enjoyed their company in their home base of Jackson, Wyoming. Mountain guide Halldór Albertsson has been a good friend since our first visit to Iceland, and between our many expeditions there he and his family have warmly welcomed Kathy and me to their home in Reykjavik. A memorable New Year's Eve dinner in Reykjavik, complete with a tour of the city's rightly famous neighborhood bonfires, fireworks, and celebrations, was a true highlight. Getting to know these guides and their families has meant a lot to me.

Because I wanted to make sure that we weren't just passing through these wonderful places, the expeditions that I organized almost always included a social impact project, such as creating a draft business plan for a nonprofit organization in the area or tackling a unique local marketing or financial problem. This entailed taking the time at the start of the expedition to visit a local organization and listen to an issue its members were facing, to think about the problem as we hiked and climbed and gathered around the fire at night, and to return at the end of the expedition to present what we thought might be helpful to them. Our participants learned a great deal about leadership and teamwork through the privilege of working with these organizations and communities.

Our project clients over the years included the Murie Center (Moose, Wyoming); Teton Science School (Jackson, Wyoming); Charture Institute (Jackson, Wyoming); Agrupación Medio Ambiental (AMA), Torres del Paine (Chile); University of Monterrey Center for Solidarity and Philanthropy—KIMAKUL Project (Monterrey, Mexico); the air–ground rescue team Flugbjörgunarsveitin í Reykjavík (Reykjavik, Iceland); United States Bureau of Land Management (Monticello, Utah); MultiKulti (Reykjavik, Iceland); Communauté d'Affaires et Tourism Stoneham (Quebec); Native American Finance Officers Association (Washington, D.C.); SEEDS (Reykjavik, Iceland); Vertical Harvest (Jackson, Wyoming); Community Rebuilds (Moab, Utah); Treefight (Jackson, Wyoming); the Village of Chinchero (Peru); WabiSabi (Moab, Utah); and rescue team Björgunarsveitin Ársæll (Reykjavík, Iceland).

To literary agents Meg Thompson and Cindy Uh at the Thompson Literary Agency in New York City, and to my editors at Praeger, Hilary Claggett and Michelle Scott, a sincere "thank you" for your support and assistance throughout the process of writing this book.

Dr. Kathy Maxwell, my wife, gamely accompanied me on almost all of the expeditions, trekking and sea-kayaking in Patagonia, canyoneering in Utah, dogsledding in Quebec, climbing and snowshoeing in Wyoming, climbing Iceland's highest peak, hiking the high trails of Peru and Nepal, and reaching the top of the Grand Teton on her fourth summit attempt in four years. This last feat was quite an emotional moment, accomplished after being beaten back once by a wild night storm and after twice putting aside her own summit climb to assist others at the Lower Saddle. Thank you for taking this incredible journey with me, Kathy.

ONE

Boots on the Ground
Developing leaders through challenging expeditions

Learning is like breathing: it involves a taking in and processing of experience and a putting out or expression of what is learned.
                                                                —ALICE Y. KOLB and DAVID A. KOLB

In the fall of 2000, while teaching an undergraduate course on leadership and teamwork at the Wharton School, I learned that Mike Useem and his colleague Edwin Bernbaum, a senior fellow at the Mountain Institute and author of the acclaimed book *Sacred Mountains of the World,* had created a leadership development program for executive MBAs and alumni that employed a most unusual and dramatic setting—the high trail to the foot of Mount Everest. Useem and Bernbaum, co-organizers and leaders of the program, had met years earlier through the Harvard Mountaineering Club, and shared a longtime interest in both mountaineering and leadership education.

In the shadow of the high snow mountains of the Khumbu region of Nepal, the Wharton Leadership Trek to Mount Everest winds through deep valleys and steep hills and across fast-moving rivers, in a long train of hikers, support staff, and yaks loaded with supplies and camp gear. Beginning at an elevation of 9,300 feet, the trek passes through the ancient trading village of Namche Bazaar and forests of rhododendron on the way to Tengboche Monastery, from where one can see the giant snow mountains Nuptse, Lhotse, Ama Dablam, and Mount Everest rising into the sky. Continuing on towards a high point of close to 18,000 feet, the trekkers pass through small villages and over swaying cable bridges, setting up a series of night camps in fields or behind ancient stone walls as the day ends.

The educational thrust of the trek draws on mountains, mountaineering, and trekking as powerful cross-cultural metaphors to expand and deepen participants' understanding of leadership and teamwork. "Images of mountains," reads the program prospectus, "resonate deeply in cultures around the world; they are symbols of patience and strength, effort and inspiration. Mountain climbers, like the mountains they climb, hold a central place in modern business and society, a paradigm for how individuals striving for a goal can achieve what others label impossible."[1]

In late April 2001, after absorbing several large stacks of pre-readings and case studies—and enduring an 8,000-mile flight—I arrived in the densely crowded and exotic city of Kathmandu, Nepal. In the confusion of the arrivals area at the airport, people of all ages held out their hands for tips as they reached for our gear and bags. Monkeys chattered and scampered along the walls outside. Trekking and mountaineering gear was scattered in large piles everywhere as groups arriving from all over the world gathered their bags and searched for rides into the city. A persistent blue haze hung over much of the ancient city, a product of the enormous number of motorcycles and vehicles on the busy streets. After an evening meeting with the other participants and a quick trip to buy some last-minute items in the local marketplace, it was on by small plane into the Khumbu region, which is the start of the Everest trail—and the leadership program itself.

The educational program of the trek emphasized continuous learning through preplanned seminars, case studies, and discussions examining the events of the day. Participants in pairs shared the leadership responsibilities for each day's travel, facilitating midday discussions and being accountable for goal setting, logistics, teamwork issues, and dilemmas—even managing personnel problems ranging from "irritation to illness."[2] After the day's trek, at the evening meal, the leaders of the day described how they had met the challenges they had experienced during the day, and the other participants offered them constructive feedback. A new pair of leaders was selected each evening, and the learning cycle began anew each morning. Each day was sure to bring an unexpected event or occurrence from which the participants were able to draw lessons about how effectively we each had—or had not—led our group over the course of the day.

On this trek, in the company of a group of mid-career professionals intensely bent on sharpening their leadership skills, I became captivated, as did many others, by the quiet yet authoritative presence of Ang Jangbu Sherpa. Ang Jangbu, one of the most experienced climbing and trekking guides in the Himalayas, summited Mount Everest in 1990 and, among his many other accomplishments, was a member of expeditions to Makalu and Dhaulagiri, the fifth- and seventh-highest mountains in the world. I followed his lead throughout the trek, observing how he smoothly organized his staff, moved fluidly on the rocky trail, and interacted with each member of the trekking party.

Ang Jangbu seemed to appear on the trail at just the right intervals, often perfectly timed to our level of exhaustion. He had the rare gifts of personal awareness and sensitivity towards others. "How are you doing, Chris and Kathy?" Jangbu would ask with a huge grin as he caught up with my wife and me resting along the trail. He'd take a moment to offer some words of encouragement and advice, warn us to be mindful of our pace, hand us each a big chunk of a Snickers bar, check

On the Everest Trek. (Photo courtesy of Michael Useem)

once again to make sure we were OK, then disappear along the trail, moving with ease and grace. His leadership style was quite different from anything I'd experienced in my professional life. He was quiet, calm, patient, thoughtful, supportive, always present and attentive, but never overpowering. I was intrigued with how he guided this large group of highly engaged, mostly type-A personalities, and his own local staff, with such quiet and easy confidence.

I learned a great deal about guides on this expedition. I learned that guides are not there to pull you up the mountain. I learned that guides honor the ground they tread. I learned that guides demonstrate the importance of respect for each other. I learned that guides show concern for their charges, and keenly sense who needs support and who can push ahead. I learned that when leading the way in difficult or unsafe conditions, guides set just the right pace, never too fast and never too slow. Most importantly, when the time and conditions are right, world-class guides encourage their teams to take the lead themselves, and create the space for participants to discover meaningful lessons on their own.

Why did management educators at a business school decide to stage a leadership development program for executives in "one of the outdoors' most stunning yet demanding classrooms,"[3] and how did that early initiative eventually lead to a program serving executive, graduate, and undergraduate students focused on learning from experience in some of the most remote and challenging areas of the world, and in close collaboration with world-class mountain guides?

I asked Useem to tell me how the program at Wharton got its start. "There were four key events," he said. "The first was the frustration that I felt in introducing the executive MBA leadership course, and coming to appreciate the limitation of a classroom for really imparting how to think about leadership, how to act as a leader, how to be strategic, how to be decisive. The classroom is great for many things, but not so much for, or not fully for, instilling basic, fundamental behavioral building blocks of leadership."

Useem began experimenting with alternatives to the traditional classroom by organizing a series of one-day trips with executive MBAs to the Gettysburg battlefield, just a few hours away from Philadelphia, walking among the monuments and event markers while considering the command decisions of generals Robert E. Lee and George Meade and others as a way for people to think about the idea of being strategic and decisive. One memorable decision point on Useem's Gettysburg tour is Little Round Top, the site on which Colonel Joshua Chamberlain, his 20th Maine troops outnumbered and out of ammunition, ordered a dramatic fixed-bayonet charge against the advancing Confederate troops, thus saving the entire left flank of the Union Army. Surveying the battlefield from the summit of Little Round Top leaves no doubt as to the importance of bold leadership decision making in crisis situations. "Somehow," Useem said, "considering the decisions made by Civil War commanders at Gettysburg as we walked the same ground was so much more memorable than anything I could have produced in the confines of a classroom."

This first effort at bringing leadership education to life in the outdoors led to the introduction in 1998 of the second initiative, the executive and alumni leadership trek to the Everest region, followed shortly by a third program for MBAs, this time a little closer to home—a guided team climb of Cotopaxi, at 19,347 feet the second-highest summit in Ecuador. Earth Treks, founded by Chris Warner, a North American mountaineer who has successfully summited both Mount Everest and K2, provided the guiding expertise and logistics for the Cotopaxi ventures.

The fourth deciding event in the creation of an expanded experiential leadership program was facilitated by several of Useem's own MBA students, including a former Army officer who was a graduate of the U.S. Military Academy at West Point and two graduates of the U.S. Naval Academy at Annapolis, both F/A-18 fighter pilots, one of whom had a fortuitous connection with the Marine Corps Officer Candidate School at Quantico, Virginia. In collaboration with Army and Marine Corps officers, Wharton leadership program participants were soon able to experience real-time decision making and teamwork while completing the leadership reaction courses—team-based problem-solving courses involving rapid decision making and physical challenge—at both West Point and Quantico.

The opportunity to make leadership decisions with real and immediate impact on a team, and to receive feedback from fellow participants, program staff, and guides, is highest during expeditions in wild and remote places. Wharton's educational expeditions differ somewhat from those of organizations like Outward Bound (OB) or the National Outdoor Leadership School (NOLS), both of which have long and very successful track records of providing wilderness leadership programs. First, unlike the open-enrollment programs offered by OB and NOLS, participants in Wharton expeditions have a preexisting educational framework in common, including prior classes in leadership and teamwork. This means that participants are primed to learn from the experience and can, as Preston Cline, director of Wharton Leadership Ventures, puts it, "go deeper faster." Secondly, Cline says, OB and NOLS expeditions follow a very specific curriculum unique to those organizations, in which the instructors are the sole sources of authority and influence. Wharton's expeditions, while encouraging participants to learn from the experience and wisdom of others whose leadership has been tested in a diverse array of situations and crises, are built around discussions facilitated by venture fellows—student leaders who are tasked with helping participants learn from the decisions they and their teams make during the day, and transfer the learning back to their educational experience. An expedition, in fact, is often just the starting point of a longer journey of discovery for many participants.[4]

Useem's bias for action and learning about leadership through experience is clear. He told me:

> I have seen dozens and dozens of company renderings of the 5 or 10 most vital qualities of leadership at a given firm, and I could make the case that if you step back and get away from the particular words, the qualities or capacities are pretty universal—strategic thinking, decisive decision-making, and persuasive communication. They're just put in different words at different companies. I think we do need a list of what really defines great individual and collaborative leadership, but we shouldn't spend too much time trying to refine it. We have just got to get going and get those competencies *strengthened*; you almost can't miss if you go for the 5 or 10 that are the most obvious. The competencies critical to have in mind, the particular way to phrase them or write them out, is less important than having the general thought behind each.[5]

McKinsey consultants Pierre Gurdjian, Thomas Halbeisen, and Kevin Lane agree: devising effective leadership development programs, they write, "inevitably means equipping leaders with a small number of competencies (two or three) that will make a significant difference in performance. Instead, what we often find is a long list of leadership standards, a complex web of dozens of competencies, and corporate values statements."[6]

To strengthen leadership competencies such as decision making and strategic thinking in practice, as Useem suggests, Wharton's leadership expeditions leverage three core elements; learning through experience, the principle of uncertainty, and after-action reviews.

LEARNING THROUGH EXPERIENCE

Alice Kolb and David Kolb, innovators in experiential learning, explain that learning is best understood as a process; that learning is the process of creating knowledge; and that knowledge is created through the "grasping and transformation of experience." This best occurs in a cycle in which the learner "touches all the bases"—*experiencing, reflecting, thinking,* and *acting.* Thus, concrete experiences become the basis for observations and reflections, which the learner distills into ideas which can be tested through new action—and the learning cycle continues, all the while drawing on the learner's own experience in adapting to the world.[7]

Wharton's leadership ventures and expeditions all draw on this primary theory of learning through experience. "The essence of the experience is for participants to make decisions of their own in a challenging environment and to reexamine decisions made by others in the same context," Useem and his co-authors Mark Davidson and Evan Wittenberg write.[8] Participants, most of whom have little or no experience in mountaineering or high-altitude trekking, move through the learning cycle at their own pace, in essence constructing new personal knowledge as they go. Kolb and Kolb point out that this experiential process stands in sharp contrast to the "transmission" model on which much of current educational practice is based.[9]

UNCERTAINTY

In his 2015 book *Nonsense,* Jamie Holmes writes, "The mind state caused by ambiguity is called uncertainty, and it's an emotional amplifier." Holmes notes that "tourism, science museums, and brainteasers testify to the extraordinary potential of ambiguity and mystery to captivate imagination," but "when we face unclear experiences beyond these realms, we rarely feel so safe."[10] Holmes's message is clear: learning to prepare for, adapt to, and learn from the unknown is important for emerging leaders. Miguel Escotet, a social scientist quoted by Holmes, argues that educating for uncertainty involves helping students be "flexible, self-critical, curious, and risk-embracing . . . the very capacities that tend to disappear when anxiety gets the better of us."[11]

About uncertainty and leadership expeditions, Useem and his co-authors write, "Participants are asked to address a number of decisions that are part of the venture's design, but numerous unanticipated decisions emerge as well, and both constitute the experience upon which the learning process is built."[12] Evan Wittenberg, now senior vice president of people at Box, an online secure content management and collaboration platform, took charge of the ventures program as soon as he graduated from Wharton, and quickly grasped that conditions of uncertainty encouraged expedition participants to make decisions with real consequence. "It was important to see what the participants actually did," Wittenberg told me, "and for them to get feedback in real time from both peers and experts. The idea was never that we'd do something without risk, as the whole point was introducing uncertainty and objective hazard into the mix to have some interesting discussions around decision making with real teeth in it. We wanted to find the right amount of risk that was tolerable and that would push the learning."

AFTER-ACTION REVIEWS

In keeping with the principles of experiential learning, participants in Wharton expeditions gather each evening in cramped tents, along with the venture fellows and professional guides assigned to each team, to discuss the events of the day in an after-action review (AAR). The AAR was described by Marilyn Darling, Charles Parry, and Joseph Moore in a *Harvard Business Review* article as "a method for extracting lessons from one event or project and applying them to others," conceived in 1981 to help army leaders adapt quickly to unpredictable situations. Darling and co-authors make it clear that an AAR is not merely a meeting, a report, or a postmortem examination. House rules for AARs in a crack military unit, they write, include *participate, no thin skins, leave your stripes at the door, take notes,* and *focus on the issues at hand.* The ultimate focus is on improving a unit's own learning—and behavior.[13] A U.S. Army publication, "A Leader's Guide to After-Action Reviews," says that because participants engaging in an AAR actively discover what happened and why, they learn and remember more than they would from a critique alone.[14]

Todd Henshaw, former director of military leadership at the U.S. Military Academy at West Point, and now director of executive leadership programs at Wharton, says the process of conducting an AAR includes four key questions:

- What did we intend to accomplish?
- What did we do?
- Why did it happen that way?
- What will we do to adapt our strategy or refine our execution?

Henshaw also says that the AAR is not merely an opportunity to focus on team performance, but can also serve as a catalyst for culture change. By setting a climate of transparency in which team members can challenge current ways of thinking and performing, teams are able to share where their own performance may have contributed to a team failure, and acknowledge the people and practices that helped create team successes.[15]

Useem and his co-authors describe a challenging leadership venture experience on Antarctica's King George Island that illustrates the effectiveness of the AAR. On the third day of their expedition, 18 participants, roped together for safety in 6-person teams, packed up their sleds and broke Camp 1, then navigated their way across a glacier toward Camp 2, three miles distant. Within the hour, all landmarks on the glacier had disappeared in a whiteout, and it quickly became evident that each team, despite their GPS devices, had drawn different conclusions about the

Expedition participants in Antarctica. (Photo courtesy of Michael Useem)

route. In the blowing snow, one team was seen heading east, another north, and a third south. The teams finally concluded that the best course was to retreat together back to Camp 1 and regroup.

Useem and his co-authors write:

> For some of the participants, it came as an unusual personal defeat: they had failed to reach a designated objective. In their young but so far successful careers, this was an unfamiliar experience. . . . As the students relived the experience in their after-action review at the end of the day, they came to better appreciate the need for an overarching decision process to resolve disagreements over direction. Though in their classroom leadership course they had all been exposed to the concept of being clear minded about one's destination before setting forth, until they experienced its tangible failure on the march up the Bellingshausen Dome, the principle had been appreciated more intellectually than behaviorally.[16]

In the following chapters, we turn our attention to two key guide organizations, Vertical and Exum Mountain Guides, to learn more about their history, guiding practices, and strengths in leadership development.

TWO

Vertical

Leveraging social skills and uncertainty

Enduring endless storms, raising tents in strong winds, battling against exhaustion, and fighting for oxygen at higher altitudes are only a part of climbing the highest mountains in the world. The true story is the people struggling to make their dreams come true.

—VERTICAL, S.A.

Guiding is not about reaching the summit. It's about deep change.

—RODRIGO JORDAN

I arrived in Santiago, Chile, on a spectacular austral summer day. The political and cultural center of Chile, Santiago is nestled in the Maipo Valley and spreads lengthwise along the Mapocho River, bordered by the attractively shaded walkways of the Parque Forestal, and encircled by the Andes to the east and the Cordillera de la Costa to the west. To the south of the river lie the most densely populated areas of the city, while to the north the Parque Metropolitano occupies the hillsides of Cerro San Cristóbal. To the east, and visible from the city in clear weather, the snow peak Cerro El Plomo rises to almost 18,000 feet.

I walked a short distance from my hotel in the Providencia district through flowering trees and past well-manicured apartment buildings, and quickly found my way to Vertical's headquarters, situated adjacent to a small park. Eugenio "Kiko" Guzman, a youthful-looking guide who has already reached the summit of Mount Everest twice, greeted me warmly at the door. Inside, Vertical's offices fairly hummed with activity. Upstairs, a psychologist and a group of program planners worked on elements of a new 360-degree feedback system for a client company. Downstairs, next to the conference room, two organizational consultants from Vertical's *Capital Humano* consulting group prepared to meet with mid-level executives of large utility company for the kickoff of a year-long leadership development training program. Tomás Grifferos, director of *Fundación Vertical*, a nonprofit foundation that delivers leadership training and capacity-building programs for youth, senior citizens, and low-income community leaders throughout Chile, had offices nearby, as did Rodrigo Jordan, Vertical's founder.

A short walk away, in the Ñuñoa district, a stately old building houses *Instituto Vertical*, a professional training institute that delivers two- and four-year instructional programs in ecotourism and sports management. Downstairs at the institute, Sergio Arraya, academic director of the school, and Felipe Estay, head of the department of eco-tourism and adventure sport careers, met with students and planned for the new semester. Upstairs, guides Guillermo "Willie" Parra, a naturalist, mountaineer, and dive master, and Gabriel Becker, a Mount Everest climber, were gathered around a table with Vertical Expeditions staff members, discussing logistics and preparing for upcoming leadership ventures to Patagonia and Antarctica.

This was clearly no ordinary guide agency.

Rodrigo Jordan, chairman of Vertical, S.A., has an extensive résumé that includes experience as a high-altitude mountaineer, guide, professor, social entrepreneur, author, and successful businessman. Jordan, who earned a PhD in innovation from Oxford University, was so committed to mountaineering that he requested and was granted permission to delay the start of his doctoral program while he made his first attempt at Mount Everest.

At Oxford, Jordan's research focused on introducing and diffusing technology designed to alleviate poverty. He told me:

> For my thesis, I traveled the world over, and researched how people introduced appropriate or intermediate technology into rural communities. I made a sort of chart which showed that if you want to be successful introducing new technology into communities, these are the things you need to check, similar to navigating when you are sailing. I realized from my research that the most successful programs were those in which the person in charge had *social skills*, more so than technical knowledge. For example, I found that for an engineer teaching the use of new technology to the Masai people of East Africa, the key to success was someone who could relate with people, not someone who would jump over thousands of years of traditions and knowledge.

This insight continues to infuse Jordan's, and Vertical's, thinking about the importance of social skills in society, mountaineering, and guiding.

Despite the extraordinary hazards, Jordan's team of Chilean mountaineers first set out to climb Mount Everest in 1986 by the North Col route, approaching the mountain from the Tibetan side. His team fell short of their goal, abandoning the attempt when one of their team members died in an avalanche. They tried again in 1989, this time by the West Ridge, without success. Jordan's team finally summited

Vertical guides teaching rappelling in Santiago, Chile. (Photo courtesy of the author)

on May 15, 1992, using a difficult and dangerous route up the Kangshung, or East Face, of the mountain, once again approaching from Tibet. The East Face is described as "nearly two vertical miles of jagged rock and black ice, a colossal challenge for surviving, let alone ascending at high altitude."[1] With this climb, Jordan's team became the first South American expedition to reach the summit of Mount Everest, and just the third expedition in history to reach it by the East Face.

On May 18, 2012, to celebrate the twentieth anniversary of his first successful climb, Jordan and a team of Vertical climbers reached the summit again, approaching from the Nepal side via the South Col route. Jordan and three Vertical team members reached Everest's summit for the third time on May 23, 2016. This third summit, accomplished via the North Col route, completed what they had set out to achieve in their first attempt thirty years earlier. To commemorate the occasion, Jordan and his team set a memorial plaque at the burial place of their fallen colleague who perished in the 1986 avalanche.[2]

As Jordan's successful climbing team was returning to Chile from the Himalayas in 1992, they made an important decision together:

We knew that we would be on the front pages of the newspaper when we got back to Santiago, and we all agreed that we should make use of this and start a foundation for taking kids up to the mountains. We climbed Everest not only because we were good mountaineers, but also because we had good social skills. Social skills are important but are rarely taught in schools. So we joined these two ideas together, taking young people into nature and building social skills.

Given his wide range of skills and enterprises and his history of high-altitude, high-stakes mountaineering I asked Jordan if he considered himself a *guide*. He said:

> I became a guide because suddenly I was teaching. I was not just leading a group of equals up a very difficult mountain like Mount Everest, I was teaching young students about hiking and camping outdoors and social skills. By pure luck, we were up in the mountains near Santiago doing a program with children and we got a call from the CEO of a large bank in Chile. I came down in shorts and mountaineering boots and went straight into the office. The CEO wanted us to develop a social skills program for the professionals in the bank. We worked with 700 people in this program. After that we started Vertical.
>
> Then something powerful happened to me. Someone I knew wanted to go to Mount Everest. I told him I thought it would take two years of his life to get ready, and he said he was willing to do so. And so we agreed, and we embarked on a strenuous training program with him, and he successfully reached the summit with our expedition. He said to me, "This is the first time in my life that I did something because I really *wanted* to, not because of business or social pressure or because I *had* to."
>
> And then the whole thing made sense. Mountaineering stopped being an end in itself and started to be a vehicle. It's not about taking someone to the summit; it's about helping someone to live an experience that will make a deep impact. So, now I proudly say, "*I'm a mountain guide.*" But it took me several years to realize that. You're a successful guide if, by the end of the trip, whether you are successful in reaching the goal or not, something deep was moved, a stone was turned, and your client develops an insight about his or her life. So when someone comes back to me after a trip and says something deeply changed in me—that's successful guiding.

Jordan summed it up: "If a guide thinks he's successful because all members of his group reached the summit, I ask, *What happened to them? Did you find out what was inside them at the end of the trip?*" I want guides to understand that their role is allowing people to gain important insights about themselves, their groups, their families, their lives. Guiding is not about reaching the summit, it's about deep change."

Beginning in 1993 with adventure-based programs for school children and summer camps, Vertical's nonprofit work, administered through Fundación Vertical, has now served over 100,000 low-income residents throughout all regions of Chile, and the programs are continuing to grow quickly through an increasing interest from both the Chilean government and from corporations committed to social entrepreneurship. "It's all about social skills," Jordan says, "the skills you need to work with other people, teamwork and leadership. It's how you are going to solve conflicts, and how you agree to disagree."

Tomás Grifferos, a physical educator and Vertical's first employee, was responsible for the health and training of the 1992 Mount Everest team. At the newly established company, Vertical, S.A., he quickly assumed charge of the efforts to bring lessons from the climbing team's experience to adventure-based educational programs for predominantly low-income school children throughout Chile. Building social skills was important, he knew, but another interesting and useful variable quickly became apparent. There simply was something different about being outside and moving freely in nature, he felt, and he knew this was quite different from the physical movements of more familiar sports that are conducted in a standardized space, such as a tennis court or a football field. Another key to developing programs for young people, Grifferos and Jordan thought, was what they sensed as the presence of uncertainty in the natural environment. "You don't always know what you're walking towards," Grifferos said, "and you don't know the outcome. Uncertainty levels out physical differences between people, big or small, fast or slow—which means that they must work together to accomplish tasks."

Uncertainty continues to be a principle that Vertical leverages in its programs today, and Jordan's guides have learned to allow it to play a key role on its educational trekking expeditions. Vertical guides teach basic camp and navigation skills to the participants, and then, rather than leading the way, often guide their trekking teams from behind. Kiko Guzman told me:

> On these expeditions, we do not lead from the front, that's true. We always tell the participants that the guides are there just in case something goes really wrong. The participants are going to make the decisions, and we will be with them all the time, but we're not going to lead them anywhere, we're there as a backup. We say, "If you get lost, we are going to get lost with you." We really do that. We try to give the client the responsibility to run the program, to be accountable.

Leadership expedition on Isla Navarino, Chilean Patagonia. (Photo courtesy of the author)

On Wharton's graduate student expeditions, venture fellows—second-year MBAs who have been trained to help coach the other participants—have made it possible for the Vertical guides to change their practice, and in so doing, to enhance the teams' experience of making decisions with real impact. Guide Gabriel Becker said:

> When we started guiding the Wharton program the guides played a double role, both guiding the teams and running the after-action reviews. Now, by training the venture fellows in advance, we have developed a communal way to allow participants to experience their own leadership and their mistakes. Things that are linked to security, those are boundaries you cannot pass. But the things that they can try, we let them, even if that means a group gets lost. As long as it's within the boundaries of safety, we are not going to say no. If they get really lost, or compromise security, the guide will take the team leader aside quietly, and ask her, *"Are you sure?"* Or the guide will ask, *"Have you seen other groups around?"*

Gaining confidence with the process as each day passes, the team's after-action review, facilitated by the venture fellow and supported by the guide, can always be counted on to sort out what happened and why, and to discover what can be learned and applied elsewhere from the decisions made by both the leader of the day and the team itself.

Vertical's work now includes a dizzying array of programs, including training teams who work in extreme operations such as mining; conducting leadership development and organizational transformation programs for corporations; sponsoring

Leadership expedition on Isla Navarino, Chilean Patagonia. (Photo courtesy of the author)

programs to support and develop entrepreneurship and social entrepreneurship; promoting the value of healthy activity in Chilean society through a national hiking program; engaging in scientific expeditions to Antarctica and Greenland; organizing private group and commercial expeditions to the Himalayas; designing and operating leadership development expeditions for universities based in the United States, Mexico, and Chile; producing books, publications, and video documentaries; and organizing an annual leadership conference in Santiago.

Jordan says,

> We're happy we've been successful in the business area. But even when we're working with the business community, we are still trying to get out our ideas about community and development. Our social work is not done only through the programs of the Foundation. Even in our business seminars, we are trying to get to this. When we define with clients what we think an exceptional team is, we say it's that you achieve something that impacts your company, your family, your community, your city, your country. That's the first element we put in. We don't define successful teams just by whatever financial results they have, but by what impact they have in their community.

Jordan's conception of the key components of leadership, which includes a "skills triangle" of technical, social, and personal skills,[3] is underpinned by values forged through long experience in extreme mountain conditions. Of being in camp after a week of pulling sledges across the snow during a challenging expedition to Antarctica Jordan writes:

> We're exhausted. The last two days have been in continuous ascent, but now the slope seems to ease. Gradually, I see the end of the valley. A massif of mountains closes the passage. It is late and there is no option but to set up camp. Terrible night. If there is no way to pass, we will have wasted food and fuel, without having made the crossing. We are completely isolated between the highest mountains of Antarctica and our survival depends solely on us. Not even a chance to think of external assistance. The next day we went out to explore and returned to the camp completely downhearted. There is no pass.

After much discussion Jordan's expedition team made a bold plan to use their climbing ropes to lower their equipment and team members down a wall of ice that fell 600 meters vertically to the next valley. Because their ropes were much shorter than the ice wall, this required a creative effort to build terraces during the descent where they could stop and recover their ropes and gear before they continued down again. After 24 hours of work they were successful and made camp for the night.

Jordan continues:

> Locked in the small tent, we slept 12 hours and then prepared dinner. The conversation drifts to the achievement and the shared feeling that we will be

able to complete the journey and face any difficulty. It is not the technical capacity or social skills of the team, which by the way are extraordinary . . . which gives us this security. What leads to this confidence is something deeper, something more substantial. I push the conversation to find out. Gradually, we got the answer—this team, like the previous ones on Everest and K2, share a code of common values. We may have differences in our personal, social, or technical skills, but all unequivocally subscribe to a set of values. For all the members, the most important thing is honesty, respect, humility, and excellence in the task.[4]

From experience gained on a scientific expedition to Greenland to monitor climate change, Jordan adds one more key value that infuses Vertical's expeditionary thinking: *generosity*.

The most important lesson we have taken from these explorations is about ourselves. It is something that bores deep into human relations. As always, to go "outside" to nature brings us, in turn, to very intimate personal introspection. Finally, what is important is not what happens "over there, outside" but rather what happens "here inside." After weeks of living with these diverse groups of people, balancing our virtues and defects, I realized that the excellent results we obtained each day were fundamentally due to the fact that we all practiced generosity daily as something intrinsically natural. Including the critical moments in which we faced a storm or in dangerous situations in which the natural tendency is "save yourself if you can," we all used our abilities for the sake of others. I am grateful to Antarctica and Greenland for showing us the best of ourselves. I ask myself whether we should not always practice this during our time on Earth. Generosity appears to be the essential ingredient for the building of shared living experiences that are rich, stimulating, welcoming, inclusive and fair . . .[5]

THREE

Exum Mountain Guides

Leadership and excellence in the home of American mountaineering

Help Wanted: Exum Mountain Guides, the country's premier climbing service, is looking for supremely talented alpinists with world-class résumés for seasonal work in the Tetons. Must be willing to follow in the footsteps of legends. If qualified, don't bother calling. We'll find you.
—KEVIN FEDARKO (*Outside* Magazine)

This is an adventure. The definition of adventure is that you don't know the outcome.
—AL READ

As winter tightened its icy hold on the high peaks of the Teton Range, I pulled into the small gravel parking area of the historic Murie Ranch in Moose, Wyoming. The 77-acre ranch is situated on the periphery of Grand Teton National Park in northwest Wyoming, bordering a curve on the Snake River, and nestled at the foot of the towering Grand Teton. I had arranged to stay at the ranch over the Christmas week to interview several senior mountain guides affiliated with Exum Mountain Guides. Other than the occasional moose crossing through the meadows of the ranch, Kathy and I were alone in the deep silence of the December snow.

The Murie Ranch was first established as a dude ranch in the 1920s. Olaus and Mardy Murie took up residence in 1946. Olaus, a noted wildlife biologist and naturalist, later became the first president of the Wilderness Society, and the ranch became the focal center of the conservation movement in the 1940s. It is now a national historic landmark. The ranch staff had asked us to snowshoe the paths between the cabins to keep them clear of deep snow during their absence, and we happily set about doing this during the day, and prepared the Homewood Cabin for meetings with the guides in the evenings.

The Grand Teton, Jackson Hole, Wyoming. (Photo courtesy of the author)

The Teton Range has long held a special place in American mountaineering history.[1] The Grand Teton, at 13,770 feet the tallest of the peaks, has drawn climbers to its summit since the late 1800s, although the date of the first ascent is still a matter of some dispute. Two members of a U.S. Geological Survey party, Nathanial Langford and James Stevenson, claimed to have reached the summit of the Grand Teton on July 29, 1872, but left no cairn or other evidence. From the descriptions Langford provided to the press, it seems more likely that they actually reached the West Summit, known as the Enclosure, which is several hundred feet below the true summit of the Grand and features distinctive slabs of granite arranged in a circle, probably an early American Indian vision quest site.[2]

Over the next two decades other climbers made a number of unsuccessful attempts at the summit of the Grand, including, in 1891 and again in 1897, climbing parties organized by William O. Owen. Finally, on August 11, 1898, Franklin Spalding, William O. Owen, Frank Petersen, and John Shive reached the top. To secure their place in mountaineering history, they climbed to the summit again two days later and made sure to document their success with a photograph and by chiseling their names on a summit rock. Despite their efforts, the controversy of who first climbed the Grand continued for years, played out in the national press—and continues to this day for some. Their summit route is now known as the Owen-Spaulding route.[3]

Former park ranger (and now Exum guide) Renny Jackson describes the Grand Teton as "one of the finest mountaineering objectives in the United States" due to the wide variety of challenging routes on its many faces and ridges.[4] Lacking any significant foothills to impede a rapid approach, the summit of the Grand, about 7,000 feet above the valley floor, is little more than three horizontal miles from the nearest approach road. The glory days of the Tetons as a proving ground for young climbers reached their peak in the 1950s; among the many alpinists who honed their climbing and guiding skills in the Tetons are Paul Petzoldt (founder of the National Outdoor Leadership School), Glenn Exum (whose name is still carried by the guide service now based in the park), and Yvon Chouinard (founder of the Patagonia clothing empire). Several members of the first American expedition to Mount Everest in 1963 were recruited from the Exum guide service.

The historic wooden headquarters of Exum Mountain Guides lies within Grand Teton National Park, nestled at the edge of an open field, just across Cottonwood Creek. Behind the cabin, a gravel road winds across Lupine Meadows to the trailhead, the main point of access for climbers who plan to scale the Grand Teton. Unassuming as it is, the cabin is a small treasure in the national park system, part of a camp erected to house workers of the Civilian Conservation Corps from 1935 until the closure of the camp in 1941. Exum, America's oldest and most experienced mountain guide service, calls this small cabin home.

On the wall of the cabin are dozens of framed photographs of Exum guides, past and present, who gaze out from high peaks around the world: men and women, tanned and fit, wearing mirrored sunglasses, some of the men bearded, and with hair of all shades from blonde to black to grey, long and short. Many are wearing colorful scarves or wool caps, and, in the newer photos, form-fitting technical soft shells and fleece, with crampons, rope, and racks of gear slung over their shoulders.

Almost 80 top mountain guides today are listed as active at Exum, and their lineage stretches all the way back to Paul Petzoldt. Molly Absolon, a NOLS instructor, writes about Petzoldt:

> Paul's first ascent of the mountain is deservedly infamous. In 1924, at the age of 16, he and his friend Ralph Herron wandered into Jackson Hole and announced they were going to climb the Grand. Their foolish bravado was met by skepticism and teasing by the locals, but Billy Owen, who is credited by some with the first ascent of the peak, took them seriously and drew a map of the route for them. Dressed in blue jeans and cowboy boots with the map in hand, Paul and Ralph set off on their adventure. Three days later, humbled, exhausted, and dressed in rags, the two straggled back to town. They had succeeded in climbing the mountain, but as Paul told reporters in the summer of 1994 at the 70th anniversary of that ascent, "It was awful. We did everything wrong . . ."[5]

Petzoldt soon befriended a young musician, Glenn Exum, who was playing in a band down at Jenny Lake and doing summer trail work in the park. From this early partnership sprang the Petzoldt-Exum School of American Mountaineering— and one very big leap of faith. On July 15, 1931, Petzoldt, who was guiding a pair of Austrian clients to the summit of the Grand Teton, directed Exum to take a look at a ledge he'd seen earlier, saying, "Why don't you go over there, take a look at that ledge, and if you think it'll go, why go, and we'll meet you on top."

Glenn Exum tells what happened next:

> That day the wind was blowing from the southwest and I got up there to the end of that ledge and it scared me, but when I called out to Paul, he couldn't hear me and didn't answer. I walked away from the ledge seven times, until I finally got up there and saw those little handholds and the boulder on the ridge. When you get to the eastern extremity of Wall Street, why, there isn't any place to jump from. So I climbed as high as I could until I was sorta secure, and I jumped from a standing start. Once I got across there, I was mortified. Almost paralyzed. But I just decided that from then on I was going to change my whole attitude about it, because there was only one way to go, and that was up.[6]

Exum, wearing a pair of football cleats two sizes too big, not only made it across the ledge, but also found a new route to the summit—and beat Petzoldt and his clients to the top by an hour and a half. To this day the route is named the Exum Ridge, one of the two main routes to the summit. Exum purchased the guide service from Petzoldt in 1956, and ran it successfully with a parade of brilliant, and often colorful, mountaineers until 1978, when he sold the business to four of his senior guides, one of whom was Al Read.

Read writes:

> Glenn had tremendous charisma and a commanding presence, but he also had an innate kindness about him. I came to admire him deeply. His presence and amazing guiding history and traditions made me want to be a mountain-climbing guide more than anything else, but I was only in my mid-teens. Still, I simply could not forget the images from reading *The White Tower,* which portrayed guiding as a demanding leadership role in the face of danger, requiring honor and self-sacrifice to protect the clients who placed their lives in trust with their guide. It seemed in my youth the most valiant and exciting of professions. After five more years of climbing, doing what were then the most difficult routes in the Tetons (mostly to impress Glenn and his guides), I finally won Glenn's trust enough that he asked me to become one of his five guides.[7]

During our talks at the Murie Ranch, Read told me:

> Exum's way is to teach clients to actually *participate* in the climb. Glenn Exum traveled to Europe in the mid-1930s to climb the Matterhorn and the Eiger, and he observed that the European guides basically guided one-on-one. Their style of guiding was to tie a rope around a client's waist—then the guide would climb up, and he would just *pull.* There was no way that the client was taught anything about climbing. Glenn came back and said wouldn't it be great to have his and Petzoldt's climbing school involved with teaching clients how to climb for a few days, so that when they are going up the Grand Teton or the other climbs, they can actually participate. And so we started doing that, and we are still basically the only mountain guide service in the United States that really does that.

To learn more about this unique approach to guiding was why I had come back out to Wyoming. I had spent some time in Jackson Hole the two prior summers and had already climbed with the Exum guides. I brought a team of Wharton undergraduates to climb the Grand Teton with Exum one summer, and that experience was so good that it turned into four summers in a row. I had already observed that the Exum guides led teams in a very specific way, teaching about leadership through both actions and words as much as they did about climbing. This winter visit gave me an opportunity to talk with the guides over the Christmas week at a more leisurely pace, and to play host in the evenings at the quiet ranch.

Read, Exum's president at the time of our talks, was instrumental in helping me reach out to eight guides who were willing to drop by the cabin, one or two each evening, for a warm drink and some straight talk about guiding. All were senior guides at Exum Mountain Guides at the time of the interviews, and all had extraordinary guiding, climbing, and expedition resumes. In addition to Read, the guides included Jack Turner, a philosopher-climber and veteran of numerous expeditions and treks in Asia, who has earned accolades for his books about the Yellowstone ecosystem, including *Teewinot: Climbing and Contemplating the Teton Range*; Jim Williams, the first to guide all Seven Summits in less than one year; Kent McBride, who serves as a ski and climbing guide around the world; Nancy Feagin, the 11th woman to summit Mount Everest; and Christian Santelices, who has big-wall first ascents in North America and Patagonia to his credit, and who with three friends (including Hans Florine, Nancy Feagin, and Willy Benegas) completed the first and only ascent of 20 of Steck and Roper's *Fifty Classic Climbs of North America* in a single 20-day enchainment.[8]

Joining them were Jack Tackle, a climber who specializes in extreme ascents in Alaska and around the world, including first ascents on Denali and expeditions to Peru, Pakistan, and Mount Everest; and Doug Coombs, who won fame as a two-time world extreme skiing champion, for his ski mountaineering exploits in the Tetons, and for his early development of steep ski camps in Alaska and the French Alps (Doug later died in a ski-mountaineering accident). At a later date, I spoke with Amy Carse, Mount Everest climber and former NOLS and Khumbu Climbing School (Nepal) instructor; Wes Bunch, who achieved a new route and first ascent on Mount Hunter and has guided on high peaks in North and South America, and expeditions in Alaska, China, the Himalayas, and Patagonia; and Mark Newcomb, who conducted the first guided ski descent of the Grand Teton with Doug Coombs, and led expeditions to remote areas of western China.

Guide Nancy Feagin told me:

> Guiding doesn't fulfill the *climbing* needs that I have, to have my heart pounding, or to be on the edge of extremes. For me, the gratification of guiding comes when I see somebody do something that they never thought they could do, or watch someone experience something that they will remember for a lifetime. The first time they do an overhanging rappel, or when someone is sure they won't make it to the top of a pitch or the top of the mountain, and then they make it—*that's* why I guide.

Exum guide Christian Santelices, whom we will meet again in the next chapter, explains why he guides, both at Exum and internationally:

> I really enjoy teaching, and I'm fascinated with cultures and natural history. I get such a thrill out of taking people and showing them new places and seeing it affect their lives. Some of those people go back home and have a better environmental approach or a better social conscience. When I take my clients out, it's not for me; it's for them. I want them to be affected by what's going on, and that requires compassion and being able to motivate people, helping them find the inspiration to do something they otherwise wouldn't do, being able to build that trust. I think that's the key.

Guide Christian Santelices sets up the 120-foot rappel on the Grand Teton. (Photo courtesy of the author)

Exum's standard four-day program for climbing the Grand Teton has been well established for many years. Climbers meet their guides on day one for a full day of training at the Exum Rocks above Hidden Peak or a short distance away at Rendezvous Peak, and work in small groups to learn climbing fundamentals including balance, technique, knots, use of the rope, belaying, and rappelling. Day two has a tougher schedule, requiring climbers to advance to steeper, multi-pitch climbs, anchored belays, overhanging rappels, and belaying the leader. Day three includes a demanding hike from the valley up to the Exum Hut at the Lower Saddle (11,650 feet) and a hurried but tasty supper of something mysteriously freeze-dried, followed by a restless sleep in the crowded shelter. Day four starts before dawn, when the guides enter the hut to boil some water for coffee, and the final ascent begins on a series of fancifully named routes to the summit. Guide Nancy Feagin says, "One guide will do the beginning class, a different one will do the intermediate class, and a third guide will do the Grand Teton with them. That way, clients will see different climbing and teaching styles, and they might learn more with a variety of different guides."

Climbers come from all over the world to climb in the Tetons. Some come with little to no experience in serious mountaineering, and they look to the expert guides—most of whom have many years of experience on the highest mountains of the world—to provide instruction and coaching as they ascend the high peaks and rock spires rising from the valley and the surrounding canyons. Other, more skilled climbers come to Exum to learn advanced techniques, challenge some of the more complex peaks, or even attempt the famed Grand Traverse, climbing several peaks in a single enchainment. Well away from all this routine activity, a few Exum guides quietly train SEALS and other special ops teams in advanced mountain techniques.

For even the novice climbers, however, the Exum guiding philosophy goes well beyond simply leading clients to the summit. Exum guides teach clients to climb the high peaks in small groups, the team rising in caterpillar fashion up the rock face. The guide, going up first, places some safety protection in cracks in the rock, which will aid in case of a fall. Each subsequent climber then takes full responsibility for the safety of the climber following below. As one climber reaches a safe place a rope length above the one below, she gathers up the remaining loose rope, tosses it to one side, takes a seated position with one leg braced against a rock, and loops the rope around her hips, thus providing a brake in case of a fall by the next ascending climber.

This is no small matter. In fact, it's very serious business: the life of the climber below is now literally in the hands of the one above. Exum teaches a very specific communication routine to all climbers. Lyndsey Bunting, a participant in two summit attempts, tells how it works:

> The sun was just coming up as we reached the first pitch. We roped in, checking our harnesses as the first of the group began to climb. I watched as my rope disappeared with Carlos along the features known as the Belly Roll and

Climbing the Upper Exum Ridge on the Grand Teton. (Photo courtesy of the author)

the Crawl. Several minutes later my rope tightened and I knew that Carlos was on belay.

"That's me, Carlos!" I yelled, trying to project my voice above the wind.

"Climb, Lyndsey!" he yelled back.

"Climbing, Carlos!"

This was the simple dialogue that we had practiced over and over in climbing school to let each other know that we were in position to accept responsibility for each other's safety. While I had just met Carlos that week, I knew that if I should slip, he would not let me fall to my death. Carlos and I practiced several of these exchanges as we slowly fought our way up the mountain. This continued down the line as the team slowly progressed towards the summit.

Exum's participative guiding philosophy transforms an exciting adventure in unfamiliar territory into a very powerful learning experience. Lessons learned when your life and the lives of your team members are on the line are likely to stick.

It didn't take me long to figure out that these extraordinary guides were demonstrating a clear set of leadership strengths that had applications to both mountaineering and business. In the years following the guide interviews, while embarking on more expeditions around the world with teams of participants and expert guides, I listened and re-listened to the many hours of taped interviews I had accumulated, and sorted through hundreds of pages of typed transcripts, circling common themes and identifying supporting quotes.

What soon became clear to me is that although the Vertical and Exum guide interviews were conducted in different countries, different hemispheres even, and guiding philosophies differed according to the design of the program and the terrain (for example, on trekking expeditions the Vertical guides often take a position toward the back of their trekking teams, thus providing opportunities for participants to discover their own path, while the Exum guides lead client teams from the front on technical climbing routes), there were remarkable similarities in the leadership strengths of the guides and their impact on the participants.

But, before we get too much further, let's follow a young big-wall climber as he starts his journey to become a world-class guide.

FOUR

The Making of a Guide

Leadership lessons from Patagonia
and the Grand Teton

Once we had everything established, we pulled up our ropes and lived on the wall for 19 days.
—CHRISTIAN SANTELICES

"It was just a small photo of a mountain tucked in the back of an obscure British journal . . ." That's how Chris Breemer, writing 20 years ago in *Climbing* magazine, described what first sparked his interest in tackling a remote rock face jutting skyward a sheer 4,000 feet near the southern tip of Chilean Patagonia.[1] Breemer's articles about the ascent in *Climbing* and the *American Alpine Journal*[2] provide us with the main thread of the narrative about this extraordinary climb. Christian Santelices, one of the three young participants on the climb, provided additional details during interviews and our many travels together in North and South America.[3] This brief story, and the one to follow, trace Santelices' path at two points in his professional development from a young climber discovering the wonders and rewards of mountaineering to an internationally certified mountain guide.

In early December 1994, Chris Breemer and two friends, Brad Jarrett and Christian Santelices, set their sights on establishing a new route on the unclimbed and "frightfully blank" east face of Cerro Escudo ("The Shield"). Breemer and Jarrett were old schoolmates who had often climbed together, scaling big walls like Yosemite's El Capitan. The pair had just won a Mugs Stump Award (sponsored by adventure gear outfitters like Black Diamond, Patagonia, and W. L. Gore & Associates, Inc., among others) to fund the expedition. Santelices, 26, had roomed with Breemer at the University of California at Berkeley, and had also worked with him at Cal Adventures at Berkeley and at the nearby City Rock Climbing Center in Emeryville. Santelices, writes Breemer, "overflowed with enthusiasm, but it was his

Looking up the Valle del Silencio to Cerro Fortaleza (center) and Cerro Escudo (right). (Photo courtesy of Nicolas Danyau)

constant friendly disposition and ability to stay psyched in freezing rain that made him ideal for the route."

Santelices, whose dream was to become a mountain guide, earned a degree in anthropology at Berkeley. He already had a remarkable climbing resume that included completing 20 classic climbs in North America in 20 days with three friends in 1993, each taking turns driving nonstop at night from one climb to the next. This feat of consecutive climbs in California, Utah, Colorado and Wyoming, which included routes on El Capitan, Castleton Tower, Long's Peak, and the Grand Teton, has not been repeated.

This would be the first climbing expedition to Patagonia for Santelices. His Chilean father owned and operated a ranch, Estancia Rio Verde, set among windblown fields close by the Straits of Magellan, just a short distance from Punta Arenas. The trip, an opportunity to combine a visit to his extended family in Patagonia with a climb of Cerro Escudo, was set.

Located in Torres del Paine National Park, Cerro Escudo rises in the Valle del Silencio, reached only by a small climber's trail. As Santelices describes it, the unclimbed wall of "amazing, beautiful rock" was both "awe-inspiring and irresistible." The face, however, was far too difficult and steep to free climb using just hands and feet. To ascend a wall like this, climbers use a technique known as aid climbing in which protective equipment (such as a piton or spring-loaded camming device) is first placed in small cracks in the rock.

To this equipment the climber clips an étrier (a webbing ladder), climbs up on the ladder as high as possible, searches for another small crack and places another piece of equipment into the rock, and attaches and climbs another set of ladders, over and over—ascending perhaps four feet at a time. The lead climber is protected from falls by the safety equipment placed into the rock, through which a rope is threaded and held by a belaying partner below. As the lead climber reaches an end point, an anchor is placed into the rock, the rope is fixed to the anchor, and the climber below ascends up the rope using a mechanical ascender device. With a new belay station thus established, the process is then repeated. Aid climbing is a slow and laborious undertaking in the best of conditions.

On December 17, 1994, Breemer wrote, "with two ropes fixed and 500 pounds (of gear) at the foot of the face," the climbers began a push for the summit. What followed were 19 continuous days of vertical climbing. The climbers each took turns ascending the rock face, fixing anchors and ropes as they went. One climber would rest below in the portaledge, a hanging sleeping platform secured to the wall by an anchor and protected from rockfall from above by a natural feature. The two others climbed above and established the route, returning to the hanging camp to take their turn to rest at intervals. Breemer called this process their "morning commute."

"We had five ropes," Santelices said. "We'd average about one pitch a day, come back down to sleep, go back up the next day and fix another rope, rappel down two ropes to rest for the night, then climb back up and repeat the process until we had all five ropes fixed." Then, taking a full day, the portaledge and the climbers' gear would be hauled up to the next station as the route was gradually established, operating essentially as a moving camp. This camp was moved three times during the ascent, "capsule style," a little over 1,000 feet at a time.

"The wall was east-facing and the prevailing winds come from the west," Santelices said, "so we were fairly protected from the wind, but not completely. We'd get these wild updrafts occasionally. It snowed pretty much every day, and there were days when it snowed a lot. You'd have to just continue on and climb through all of that. In Patagonia you can get all four seasons in a day."

"Hanging beneath the portaledge in a hammock," Breemer wrote, "I felt weightless as the billowing rainfly lifted me. Cowering in my first Patagonian tempest, with my stomach turning, I wondered if the wind would gather strength and tear off our rainfly. I pulled my balaclava down farther. Ice melted on my face."

Climbing on the wall continued slowly, sometimes advancing just three pitches over the course of several days. Shortly after Christmas Day, Santelices reached a narrow, broken ledge and searched for an anchor so he could fix the ropes and rappel down to the portaledge. Breemer, belaying him from 165 feet below, waited impatiently. A sharp metallic crack told Breemer that Santelices was drilling into the rock wall.

"Christian nudged a bolt in the hole," Breemer wrote, "but as he drove it home it jammed and bent over. The hole was too small. The bolt was worthless. I remained silent, wondering if he would throw up his hands, untie, and jump. But that isn't

Christian's style. He is strong and stocky, willing to endure whatever is thrown at him. I knew he would find a way to anchor the ropes, and would be back in the portaledge with a big grin on his face. Composing himself, Christian drilled another hole, deformed another bolt, bashed a few pins into a rotten seam, tied everything together, clenched his teeth and rappelled."

Soaked and shivering from the cold, Breemer and Santelices arrived back at the hanging camp only to find that Jarrett had fallen asleep and had accidentally left the shelter's rainfly slightly open all day. Breemer's sleeping bag, the only source of comfort and warmth after hours on the freezing climb, now floated in a pool of ice water.

"Sprawled in a sodden pile of nylon, Gore-Tex, and fleece," wrote Breemer, "I was near tears and wanted to wring Brad's neck. Our sanctuary, the warm, dry home that had kept life on the wall tolerable, was now just another agent of torture." Santelices and Breemer resigned themselves to a miserable night as Jarrett, in the hammock hanging below the portaledge, dealt with the wet bag, wringing out as much of the water as he could.

Yet when the bag was handed back up to the two exhausted climbers above, it was completely dry. "Racked with guilt, and in his typical selfless style," Jarrett had handed over his own, dry sleeping bag to his partners.

In the following days, the climb continued inexorably. The three climbers were alone on the wall, the wind howling all around them. The cold, exhaustion, and monotony were beginning to take their toll. Breemer describes the feeling: "It wasn't the shivering or numb fingers that I really hated, but the gloom and despondency that the cold generated. It sucked away my motivation, left me hollow, and thinking of nothing but escape to the ground. It was a terminal disease."

Santelices was now thinking about an escape from the wall, too. He told me:

While you are leading a climb and actively climbing, all your focus is on what you are doing. You might be scared, but it's also the time of greatest focus, and you're least likely to be thinking of anything else—like home. But things start creeping into your mind when you're just hanging out in the portaledge on your rest day, or when you're belaying. Belaying in particular is difficult, because you are by yourself with your thoughts, often hanging uncomfortably in your harness in the rain and snow. Those times of inactivity are when your mind can wander and you don't want to be there anymore. Doubts come into your head. You are where you are and there isn't anything you can do to change it. I just really wanted to go home. The weather was bad, we were stuck there on the wall, and when you're left to your own thoughts, well, things start to fester. The more time you spend hanging around doing nothing, the more time you have for your thoughts to turn on you.

"Sixteen days on the wall now," Breemer wrote, "the junk food, beer, and batteries gone. We were cooked and worried that the meager five gallons of water we had left wouldn't last the final 1,000 feet to the top and the 4,000 feet back down. We were yearning for the flatlands. None of us had ever spent so much time on a wall."

Santelices finally told the others that he wanted out. Searching for ideas, he said first he thought he might have a trekking client coming, and then that his girlfriend was supposed to show up soon. "This was my ploy to have them say, 'You know, Christian, maybe you should just go down!' You think about all the wonderful things you have at home, your family and relationships. I had a whole plan for this. I told them, 'Look, I'll just take two ropes, you can keep three ropes, I'll take my stuff, you don't have to deal with it, and I'll just go down.'"

At the same time, Santelices imagined what his two teammates were thinking about his escape proposal: "Christian gets a rope stuck, and we have to go rescue him. He takes two of our ropes, so we're up here longer, then we run out of food . . ."

"Of course, they also knew me well enough that it was quite clear that going down wasn't really a possibility," Santelices said. There would be no easy way down, for each needed the other two to complete the route.

The trio continued climbing.

Things soon began to turn around. "As if sensing our need for haste," Breemer wrote, "the crack systems improved. Our dream appeared soon to be reality . . ." Close to the summit ridge now, Santelices stopped at a ledge marking the junction between Escudo's solid granite and its shattered dark sedimentary caprock.

"The sun had set and we were too high above our portaledge to fix ropes and descend to it," wrote Breemer. "We were committed. Darkness enveloped Escudo and we each retreated to the small independent worlds of our headlamps."

Breemer traversed over Santelices and Jarrett on a thin layer of snow overlying the steep rock.

My picks uselessly slipped through the snow, and the shafts bounced off the underlying rock. I anxiously tried to jab a picket into the snow but it too glanced off rock. I considered backing down, and almost convinced myself that the climbing was really over, that the wall was done and to turn back now would still be a success. Deep down in my gut, though, I knew it wasn't over. Finally, I planted both axes in a small cornice and carefully stepped onto the summit ridge.

To the left, the ridge of rotten rock and snow continued to Escudo's summit. But by this time, Breemer acknowledged:

We were done. The wall was climbed and we had no desire to slap the summit. All I knew for certain was that this dream was nearly over, and as soon as the experience had metamorphosed into fond memory I'd be back on another cold and dripping wall, heading toward another barren summit, pursuing another dream.

Their route on Cerro Escudo, *The Dream*, is now considered by some to be Chile's most difficult big-wall route.[4]

Fast-forward now another 12 years to a beautiful summer's day, Thursday, August 17, 2006. Eight young climbers and several guides have worked their way up from the Jackson Hole valley along a steadily inclining seven-mile approach trail passing through Garnet Canyon and up onto the Lower Saddle of Wyoming's 13,770-foot Grand Teton. The team has gained almost 5,000 vertical feet over the course of the approach hike.

At 11,650 feet, the Lower Saddle is situated between the two imposing peaks of the Middle Teton and the Grand Teton. Save for a narrow level band on which the Exum Hut and a weather station sit, the fragile alpine vegetation and scattered rock surface of the saddle slopes steeply away on one side to Idaho and on the other to Wyoming. The Lower Saddle is where many climbers rest overnight as they prepare for a summit attempt early the next morning.

At 5:00 p.m. on August 17, the temperature in the valley below was a perfect 73 degrees Fahrenheit. At the Lower Saddle, the mercury had already dropped to 46 degrees. By the 3:00 wake-up call the next morning, the temperature on the Lower Saddle would fall to 37 degrees, and at the summit it would be right around the freezing point.

The Lower Saddle: To the left is the west summit and to the right is the main summit of the Grand Teton. In the right foreground is the Middle Teton. (Photo courtesy of the author)

Christian Santelices and Amy Carse, a guide with first ascents in Peru and Nepal to her credit, and who reached the summit of Mount Everest in 2004, were the lead Exum guides. Carse leaned in to talk with Santelices at the Lower Saddle. Both were now tightly focused in on one of the climbers, a young Chinese woman named Yang Sun. She had shown that she had the stamina to reach the Lower Saddle, but could she make the summit climb safely? Even the smallest issue or delay on the route can add to the risk of the climb. The Grand is notorious for frequent summer thunderstorms and lightning strikes, and reaching the summit early is vital.

Yang described some of the challenges she had experienced in the climbing school program she had completed immediately before the summit attempt. "I found myself on a rock with an incline of 60 degrees, my hands desperately trying to grab any handles possible. Every time I wanted to move a step forward, the decision took minutes. My legs were shaking violently. 'Trust your shoes!' guide Angela Hawse suddenly shouted to me. 'Stand up! Lift your hands from the rocks! Try walking, not climbing!'"

Guide Carse was particularly fierce on issues of risk and readiness when it came to her team of climbers, and she had already made her expectations clear to Yang and her teammates during climbing school. "When you say 'Climb!' you are entering a contract that promises your partner you will focus 100 percent of your attention on belaying and you will be 100 percent responsible for his or her safety," Carse said. "Never say 'Climb!' when you are not ready!"

At the Lower Saddle Carse told Yang Sun that she did not think she should attempt the summit. Although Yang felt comfortable after eight hours of hiking to the Lower Saddle, she knew that she had revealed a lack of experience and skill on the steep rocks in the previous day's climbing school. Carse wanted Yang to demonstrate her competence once again. "Amy brought up the challenge," Yang said, "saying I had to show her she was wrong by climbing some of the rocks near the Lower Saddle, following her, and following her closely." It was a hard challenge. The rocks were rough and Carse moved fast.

Yang passed the quick test Carse gave her on the Lower Saddle; in fact, she fought back hard to stay on the climb. But Carse, a very seasoned judge of ability, still had her doubts about Yang after the challenge.

After double-checking harnesses and headlamps and readying their summit packs, the team ate a quick meal and retired early that night, squeezing into sleeping bags in the crowded Exum Hut. With only a few hours to go before dawn and the summit climb, the group fell asleep quickly.

Overnight, guides Santelices and Carse resolved the issue of where Yang would climb. "Amy made her decision about where Yang should go," Santelices said, "and it was based on safety. We had enough guides to be able to do the summit of the Grand with the larger group and still be able to split up, so we agreed that I would guide Yang."

At the 3:00 a.m. wake-up call Santelices drew Yang aside, saying, "I want you to reach the summit that's best for you."

Yang Sun and Christian Santelices on the west summit of the Grand Teton. (Photo courtesy of the author)

Yang Sun, PhD. (Photo courtesy of Yang Sun)

As the team members left the tent one by one and met up outside with their ascent guides, headlamps switched on and backpacks and harnesses ready, Yang posed for a picture with Santelices and listened as he explained their plan. The whole group moved together up the first stages of the rocks above the Lower Saddle, heading for the Upper Saddle and the route towards the summit of the Grand. Then Yang set off with Santelices, scrambling past the Black Dike, up the Briggs Slab to the Black Rock Chimneys, towards the Upper Saddle, from where the route splits off to the western spur of the Grand and its summit, known as the "Enclosure." At 13,280 feet, just under 500 feet below the summit of the Grand, the massive buttress boasts the second-highest summit in the Teton Range.

As the sun rose higher in the sky, the pair finally reached the Enclosure. As they looked over to the Grand they could see the rest of the group on the Owen-Spaulding route on their final approach to the summit. The climbers on the Grand could now see and wave at Santelices and Yang Sun, both bathed in spectacular early morning alpenglow. The teams happily called out congratulations to each other across the Upper Saddle.

Yang Sun, still full of grit and determination, soon graduated summa cum laude from Wharton, and a few years later reached yet another personal and professional summit, completing her PhD in Financial Economics at MIT. She is now an assistant professor of finance at the University of Hong Kong, with a joint appointment in the school of economics and finance and the school of business.

In the following chapters, we will return to some of the key moments in Christian Santelices' Cerro Escudo climb and Yang Sun's journey on the Grand Teton. We will cover the importance of *social intelligence* to the development and maintenance of positive relationships. We'll consider how the use of a variety of *leadership styles* can have a significant impact on how people work together, and how *empowerment* can provide the space for personal growth and development. We'll revisit the need for *trust* in tough situations, and how a guide leads effectively in an environment of *risk and uncertainty*. Finally, we will show the importance of seeing *the big picture*, and how the journey to the summit is as important, if not more than, the need to "slap the summit."

Let's take a closer look now at the full set of leadership strengths of a guide, how others have applied them, and how they can be applied in your own life.

FIVE

Guides Are Socially Intelligent

The importance of building and maintaining positive relationships

If social intelligence is your top strength, you are aware of the motives and feelings of other people. You know what to do to fit into different social situations, and you know what to do to put others at ease. You are kind and generous to others, and you are never too busy to do a favor. You enjoy doing good deeds for others, even if you do not know them well.

—VIA INSTITUTE ON CHARACTER

Being a successful leader does not require directing others or taking part in every minute detail, but rather simply being aware of others and their actions and understanding where they're coming from.

—EXPEDITION PARTICIPANT

World-class mountain guides hone the intricacies of their craft through many years of experience in the most challenging of circumstances, and from lessons learned from interactions with hundreds of fellow climbers and clients. Climbing in such intense environments demands the ability to establish and maintain personal relationships that don't fracture easily under pressure.

Although all three of the climbers we met on the sheer wall of Cerro Escudo were relatively young, still in their mid-twenties, they were quite experienced mountaineers, used to climbing with partners, and could anticipate what difficulties to expect while ascending the rock face. Recall from our story in Chapter 4 that Christian Santelices and Chris Breemer's climbing partner, Brad Jarrett, accidentally left the tent fly open while he slept, allowing rain to soak his teammate's sleeping bag. When Santelices and Breemer descended from their climb and arrived at the sleeping platform fixed to the rock face, there was disappointment but little fuss. Without prompting, Jarrett handed up his own dry sleeping bag to his fellow climbers as a mindful apology for his failure to protect their gear from the ice and rain. A strong sense of self-awareness, as well as skill at sensing others' emotions, goes a long way toward building and preserving positive relationships when the chips are down.

A measure of social intelligence also likely helped Santelices' climbing mates handle his momentary wish to descend from the wall, read his emotions accurately, and formulate and communicate the appropriate response—*Christian, steady yourself. You are a key part of this team and we need you.* For his part, Santelices braced himself and avoided what Daniel Goleman calls an "emotional hijacking," a neural takeover that originates in the amygdala, a center in the limbic brain, and quickly "recruits the rest of the brain to its urgent agenda."[1]

Santelices also reflected on his own need for self-awareness, saying later, "I learned that it's important to know your own disposition, and that you may have to adjust your style. If you're with people for six weeks in really difficult circumstances, you need to know that you won't have arguments when you're in challenging situations. And, perhaps most importantly, it's important to be able to talk gracefully and intelligently about your concerns when you're in a tough place."

Participant Reflections

- At the summit of Cody Peak, a few people were already out of water and we had another long walk down the mountain. Those with extra water were gladly willing to sacrifice, and without a word an unorganized game of musical chairs with half-empty bottles of water provided everyone with a sufficient amount for the journey. Halfway down, one of my teammates felt shaky and stopped. Before the news reached me, a group of supporters had formed around her, giving her water and the encouragement she needed to proceed. At the foot of the mountain (with the end in such clear sight!) another teammate slipped on the gravel, her knees a bloody mess. A makeshift medical team quickly formed around her, and she was bandaged and walking before she had lost step with the rest of the group. *(Grand Teton Mountaineering)*

- The defining moment for me came on the evening before our summit push, as the sun was setting and the temperature was dropping on the Lower Saddle. We were set to wake up at 3 a.m. the next morning and everyone was a little nervous and on edge. The guides informed us that the team might split up, with one group attempting a longer ascent and a second team approaching the summit on a different route. I was in favor of splitting up because I was in the group that was chosen for the longer ascent. But the trip leader made the decision that there was no way the group would split up. I approached him privately and had a somewhat heated conversation, letting my desire be known. We had an open conversation about the advantages and disadvantages of each approach. In the end he made the final decision that we would all take the same route, and it was out of my hands. I am grateful that he made that decision, because in the end the most rewarding aspect of the trip was that we were able to make it up together as a team and share in the sense of our collective accomplishment. Reflecting on that conversation has taught me what it really means to be both a leader and a member of a team. *(Grand Teton Mountaineering)*

- All of a sudden I found myself at the back of the "slow" group, something I had not expected at all. Our guide stayed at the back with me, yet he did much more than just accompany me. During the time we were together, in the most modest, simple and friendly way imaginable, he instructed me how to walk more efficiently on the trail. He put particular emphasis on the fact that this was not because I was weak but rather because I was inexperienced. With his help I managed to pace myself to an enjoyable rhythm. I believe that he patiently walked with me for so long and engaged in conversations that would interest me because he was vicariously experiencing the trail through my eyes. Because he empathized with me I paid more attention to his actions. I think that this signifies how important it is to approach people with empathy while making an effort to exercise any form of leadership. *(Peru)*

Guides consistently interact with clients in a manner that demonstrates both emotional and social intelligence. Psychologists Peter Salovey and John Mayer define *emotional intelligence* as "The ability to monitor one's own and others' feelings and emotions, to discriminate among them, and to use this information to guide one's thinking and actions."[2] Management professors Sigal Barsade and Donald Gibson tell us that emotions "create and sustain work motivation. . . . they lurk behind political behavior; they animate our decisions; they are essential to leadership." Emotional intelligence is a skill in which emotions are treated as valuable data in navigating a situation, and includes perceiving, using, understanding, and managing emotions.[3]

Social intelligence was first defined in 1920 by Edward Thorndike, a Columbia University psychologist, as "the ability to understand and manage men and women, boys and girls—to act wisely in human relations."[4] Chris Peterson and Martin

Seligman, luminaries in the field of positive psychology, help bring emotional and social intelligence into focus:

> There also exists a group of hot intelligences, so called because they process "hot" information: signals concerning motives, feelings, and other domains of direct relevance to an individual's well-being and/or survival. . . . Emotional intelligence concerns the ability to use emotional information in reasoning. Personal intelligence involves accurate self-understanding and self-assessment, including the ability to reason about internal motivational, emotional, and, more generally, dynamic processes. Social intelligence concerns one's relationships with other people, including the social relationships involved in intimacy and trust, persuasion, group memberships, and political power.[5]

People who are high in hot intelligence, Peterson and Seligman say, are able to understand and manage emotion (emotional intelligence), accurately assess one's own performance at a variety of tasks (personal intelligence), and act wisely in relationships and use social information to get others to cooperate (social intelligence).[6]

Guides understand that they must get to know their clients quickly, and must build relationships that will work as the challenges of the day get tougher. "I'm a good listener," Exum guide Jack Tackle told me. "I can tell within a few minutes how it's going to go." According to Exum's Al Read, a mountaineer with wide experience on big peaks,

> You have to have people skills. The guiding job starts in the valley, even though you're just walking on the trail. As a guide, I hope that I can, in the course of the lead-up to the climb and on the approach, get to know clients well enough, to watch their traits, so I can keep them safe. You know that they are all anxious, but you watch them and test them all the way, to see if they are winded, if they have their wits about them, what their physical condition is.

Exum guide Nancy Feagin says,

> I want to have conversations at lower elevations, when the clients are feeling good, get a feel for their personality, how they walk and how they move. On the Grand Teton, guides are supposed to be at the front of the pack, but we take breaks and talk to everybody individually. If we start to worry about somebody, we talk to other people within the group to try to get a feel for if that's normal for the person or not. People listen if they are spoken to truthfully. Guides have to be insightful, able to read their clients, know when they are tired and hungry and when to push them and when not to push them, to tell when they have had enough. Sometimes people need a little more positive pushing, and sometimes they just need to go back.

Participant Reflections

- One leadership quality of the guide that aided the team tremendously was his patience. For the entire duration of the trip, I never observed him become impatient or rush anyone along, even if we were in a difficult situation or other team members were getting frustrated. While rappelling down from the rocks, I remember becoming panicked and unsure of myself. Through his guidance and patience in telling me what I needed to do, I was able to refocus and think more clearly about the task at hand. In addition, he was never overbearing or portrayed himself as superior, even though he was a renowned guide. While on the hikes and during meal times, I was able to relate to him through his stories and his easygoing nature. He asked us questions and genuinely seemed to want to get to know us. As a consequence, I was more willing to listen to him and be receptive to anything he asked us to do. The guide allowed every participant to grow individually, but was always there when we needed advice or guidance. He recognized our need to experiment and try things out on our own. Because he didn't force us to do things a certain way, I trusted that he had my best interests at heart and if I needed to, I could go to him with any questions or concerns I had without hesitation. He showed that being a successful leader does not require directing others or taking part in every minute detail, but rather simply being aware of others and their actions and understanding where they're coming from to earn their trust and respect. *(Utah)*

- A person who exemplifies leadership is one who inspires others to be better, and that's exactly what the guide did. He was dedicated to the group, and made sure that everyone's needs were met. He would be the first to rise and serve others, but the last to eat and sleep. His actions, though simple, were memorable, and his example has inspired me to be a better role model by living it in everything I do and say. *(Utah)*

- Along with trust, our guides also helped our team build listening skills. Listening is an act of respecting the intelligence of the speaker. Throughout the journey, you come to cherish the conversations that you have with others and even with yourself. The nature of hiking furthermore demands that you listen to your surroundings, your fellow hikers, and the sound of your own footsteps. Perhaps unbeknownst to anyone, listening became one of the most active forms of communication on the trek. We can't ever listen enough. When we are able to trust and listen to one another, a sense of positivity germinates and lifts us along the way. *(Iceland)*

Vertical's Rodrigo Jordan provides another perspective from experience climbing on Mount Everest and other high peaks:

You need time together. When we're forming a team for an expedition we go out climbing together months in advance. We are not only training physically and technically, but also as a team. When difficult situations arise, the leader can say, "Guys, do you realize this is happening? How can we deal with it?" The team can come up with a system for handling conflict, because on the expedition we're going to face avalanches, we're going to face hardships—and we're also going to face conflict. Usually, nobody is thinking about *human relations* on a mountaineering expedition. People are concentrating on logistics and supplies and technical skills. But it's one of the bullet points you need to deal with before the expedition starts.[7]

Expedition Behavior

Paul Petzoldt described expedition behavior in *The Wilderness Handbook* in 1974: "Human nature influences the success or failure, comfort or discomfort, safety or danger of an outdoor experience as much as equipment, logistics, trail techniques, rations, or other basic organizational concerns. . . . In high altitudes or during adventuresome, energy-draining endeavors, outdoorsmen must make a concerted effort for the consideration of companions in addition to securing their own personal comfort and safety. . . . Good expedition behavior is an awareness of the relationship of individual to individual, individual to the group, group to the individual. . . . it is this awareness, plus the motivation and character to be as concerned for others in every respect as one is for oneself."[8] Mark Harvey, a National Outdoor Leadership School instructor, writes, "Petzoldt concluded that good or bad expedition behavior often determined a group's destiny even more than technical skills or physical strength." After basic needs are met (food, water, shelter, and a sense of security), good expedition behavior springs from "all the most decent of human traits: respectfulness, flexibility, tolerance of others, courtesy, politeness, direct communication, self-awareness, open-heartedness, teamwork, sharing, and selflessness."[9] John Kanengieter and Aparna Rajagopal-Durbin, writing in the *Harvard Business Review*, remind us that empathy and communication are at the core of expedition behavior. In the backcountry we might call it expedition behavior; at home or at work, the same basic concepts are called social intelligence.[10]

Psychologist Daniel Goleman says social intelligence is what transpires as people interact, reaching beyond narrow self-interest and to the best interests of others—capacities that enrich personal relationships like empathy and concern.[11] In a recent *Harvard Business Review* article, Goleman and co-author Richard Boyatzis, a professor of organizational behavior at Case Western Reserve University, write, "The salient discovery is that certain things leaders do—specifically, exhibit empathy and become attuned to others' moods—literally affect both their own brain chemistry and that of their followers."[12] Importantly, according to Goleman and Boyatzis, "leaders' emotions and actions prompt followers to mirror those feelings and deeds. . . . Leading effectively is, in other words, less about mastering situations, or even mastering social skill sets, than about developing a genuine interest in and talent for fostering positive feelings in the people whose cooperation and support you need."[13]

Guide Christian Santelices says, "If a client doesn't have a good time, or has trouble with a skill, my first reaction is to think about how I could have improved that situation, what I missed, how I could have taught them differently. I think that's the key. It requires compassion and being able to motivate people, being able to help them find the inspiration to do something they wouldn't be able to do otherwise, genuinely caring."

Participant Reflections

- From the beginning we could see that our guides worked well together as guides, and as friends too, so it was easy to feel confident in their leadership. I can't imagine working in a successful organization whose members don't provide positive reinforcement for each other. During each day of the trip somebody would express excitement, or smile, or comfort another who felt too exhausted to move. For instance, when a team member couldn't find her harness, everybody reassured her that she would find it somewhere in her pack, which preserved team morale at a point when the wind hit even harder and our clothes got even wetter. Moments such as this inspired me to push forward, and reminded me of the beauty of overcoming a challenge in a team environment. I finally came to appreciate the guide's sentiment when he said that enjoying the hike is the most important part of it all. This intuition is part of me now, inseparable from the miles that I walked and the camaraderie of those who helped me there. *(Iceland)*

- Leadership requires empathy. On a superficial level, this means that the leader should have the ability to connect with all team members quickly and meaningfully. Furthermore, the leader should also be equipped with the understanding that everyone comes from a unique background and has had varying degrees of experience with the tasks at hand. Thus, the expectation of each member's performance and the approach which the leader adopts to interact with each team member needs to be customized accordingly. *(Utah)*

- By far, the most important lesson that I learned about leadership is the need to be attentive to and perceptive of the capabilities of others. In the context of the physically challenging hikes and climbs, each participant had varying levels of athleticism and abilities to complete these activities; some could handle the challenges fairly easily while others needed to concentrate more. During the trip, I found that the best leaders of the day were the ones who recognized the individual differences. They made sure that each participant was keeping up and more importantly, despite these differences, ensured that the hikes were finished as a team. *(Utah)*

"Over time I've developed a sense of what people's skills and talents are after working with them for just a few hours," reports Exum's Mark Newcomb. "Then I can start to help them find their role in the process, help them gel as a team. I can also give them some things they can work on to round out their skills and apply their strengths. The guide needs to understand who is best at certain skills so you can let them do that and step back and not have to micromanage them, because you're going to have other issues to deal with."

In Practice

Christian Hoogerheyde, a project manager at Socrata, a cloud software company, was a participant on an expedition in Iceland, successfully reaching the summit of the country's highest peak, Hvannadalshnúkur, with his team. "A highly-valued skill in the consulting world," he says, "is the ability to interact comfortably with people in any type of organization, no matter their function, rank, or location."

"Consultants are taught to speak a client's language and to lock in quickly to a client's culture and unique concerns as a way to earn trust. The ability to quickly establish positive relationships is crucial in this highly competitive industry. Our guide, Halldór Albertsson, received a group of clients with experiences and backgrounds vastly different from his own, and he needed to garner their trust quickly." Hoogerheyde says that Albertsson was "skilled at establishing positive relationships with each of us, and this has served as a lesson to me every time I try to earn a new client's trust. I now see firsthand how far social and emotional intelligence go towards achieving business success, and I am thankful for the example of a guide who showed me the way."

The Message

Take a cue from guides and leverage your strengths in social intelligence to establish and maintain positive relationships. Guides tune in to their clients' emotions and feelings, and put what they learn to good use as they build relationships that help their clients feel at ease in highly stressful situations. Imagine that you are on a lengthy and challenging expedition with people you are just getting to know, or that you are beginning a new project at work with unfamiliar colleagues. What kind of relationships will you build with your travel or work partners? Read through some of the action steps that follow for some advice on building strengths in social intelligence.

ACTION STEPS FOR BUILDING SOCIAL INTELLIGENCE

Daniel Goleman says social intelligence includes two main categories: *social awareness* (what we sense about others), and *social facility* (what we then do with that awareness). Social awareness includes sensing, feeling, and understanding emotional signals; mindful listening; and "knowing how the social world works." Social facility includes interacting smoothly at the nonverbal level, presenting ourselves effectively, influencing social outcomes, and showing concern for others.[14]

Consider these action steps to help you build social intelligence:

- **Learn to be a great listener.**
  - Management consultant Marshall Goldsmith says you can build skills in listening, an important component of social intelligence. Try this brief exercise: count slowly to 50 with your eyes closed and *don't let another thought intrude into your mind*. Most people find it really challenging. Practice this exercise, Goldsmith suggests, and once you can get to a count of 50 without stray thoughts interrupting, see how it can help you focus—really focus—on listening to the person you are with. Just listen. Don't interrupt. Don't finish

the other person's sentences. Don't let your attention or your eyes wander. Ask questions that show you're paying attention. Goldsmith says, "Your only aim is to let the other person feel that he or she is important. If you can do that, you'll uncover a glaring paradox: the more you subsume your desire to shine, the more you will shine in the other person's eyes."[15]

- **Respond positively and constructively to someone's good news.**
  - Shelly Gable, a professor at UCLA, and her colleagues say research has often asked, *What can people do when things go wrong?* Gable and her team looked at the other side of the equation, investigating what happens when people share, and respond to, *positive events.* Citing research that positive events are associated with well-being and health and decreases in depressive symptoms, Gable proposes that telling others about positive events can generate additional benefits by fostering positive social interactions—as long as the listener's response recognizes and validates the good news. Gable and associates suggest that responses perceived to be active and constructive were associated with emotional well-being and better relationship quality, whereas responses perceived to be destructive or passive were negatively associated with these outcomes.[16]

- **Help others feel safe.**
  - Michelle McQuaid, an Australian workplace researcher trained in applied positive psychology, says you can develop skills in social intelligence by noticing when other people around you are experiencing stress or uncertainty. Consider the emotions they might be feeling and why they are experiencing them. Slow down to help them express and work through their uncertainty more comfortably and productively.[17]

- **Trust the other person first.**
  - Social psychologist Heidi Grant Halvorson says we have a deeply rooted tendency toward reciprocity, and are naturally inclined to want to do favors, give gifts, and work to promote those who have done these things for us in the past. We are more likely to feel like we can trust someone who has trusted us first. Halvorson suggests that allowing yourself to be a bit vulnerable projects warmth and shows your human side. The perceiver, she says, is likely to feel that this invites intimacy and shows that you are players on the same team.[18]

- **Build capacity for social perceptiveness into your teams.**
  - Thomas Malone, head of MIT's Center for Collective Intelligence, says *social perceptiveness* is a kind of social intelligence. "It's the ability to discern what someone is thinking, either by looking at their facial expression or through some other means of human observation. When it comes to the effectiveness of groups, we are what we see in each other." Women are more likely to be socially perceptive than men, which is why Malone and his co-investigators suggest that the higher the proportion of women on a team, the more likely it is to exhibit what they call "collective intelligence." Malone's team found that "a group is more collectively intelligent if the people in it are, on average,

more socially perceptive—that is, if they are good at reading emotions from other people's eyes.[19] *Tip:* You can check your own level of social perceptiveness in a short online test: http://socialintelligence.labinthewild.org/mite/

- **Build a culture of "compassionate love" in the workplace.**
  - Does your workday start with a barrage of work-related questions from your colleagues, or with cheerful greetings from co-workers and an offer to grab a quick cup of coffee before the day gets into high gear? Wharton management professor Sigal Barsade says there is reason to believe that the latter scenario—which illustrates what she refers to as "compassionate love" in the workplace—is vital to employee morale, teamwork and customer satisfaction. Compassionate love is shown "when colleagues who are together day in and day out ask and care about each other's work and even non-work issues," Barsade says. "They are careful of each other's feelings. They show compassion when things don't go well. And they also show affection and caring— and that can be about bringing somebody a cup of coffee when you go get your own, or just listening when a co-worker needs to talk." Barsade suggests that tenderness, compassion, affection and caring matter at work. "Managers should be thinking about the emotional culture," she says. "It starts with how they are treating their own employees when they see them. Are they showing these kinds of emotions? And it informs what kind of policies they put into place. This is something that can definitely be very purposeful—not just something that rises organically."[20]

SIX

Guides Are Adaptable

Using the right leadership style at the right time

No one's a leader if there are no followers.

—MALCOLM FORBES

The leader must first take charge and set a pace, but also allow for the individual challenge of calculation and improvisation.

—EXPEDITION PARTICIPANT

Christian Santelices' momentary thought that he should escape from the Cerro Escudo climb could easily have precipitated an angry outburst from his climbing mates or a demand from one of the more experienced big-wall climbers that he stay put. Instead, when his climbing partners responded to his wish to descend with empathy rather than anger, they also demonstrated an ability to choose thoughtfully among leadership styles. Given the high levels of exposure and stress that each climber faced on the wall for days at a time, the lack of warmth and comfort, and the cramped and wet conditions in the hanging camp, using what Daniel Goleman calls an "affiliative" style[1] was the right choice to preserve the intense personal relationships that the climbers had built over the lengthy climb.

Guides and Leadership Styles

Guides employ a number of different leadership styles while helping clients to manage difficult terrain and reach for their summits. Support for the client's self-development, encouraging and empathetic, was a common theme that I found in the transcripts from my guide interviews. In practice, this approach is often expressed through an affirming and coaching leadership style. Guides, however, aren't shy about switching to a more directive style when conditions call for it.

Gaston Rébuffat, a key member of the French team that famously first reached the summit of Annapurna, writes:

> People have a fixed idea of what a guide is: a professional, who, in return for a certain sum of money, takes you to the summit to which you aspire. But the guide is more than that: he is a competent friend who controls the party, but who also teaches you and stimulates your interest.[2]

While all guides try to help clients along a path of self-discovery and accomplishment, building on their strengths and coaching and teaching on the finer points, guiding in the most severe environmental conditions can quickly become a *follow me* or even a *do what I tell you* process. Daniel Goleman terms the former an "authoritative" leadership style, and the latter a "coercive" style, useful but best reserved for a crisis situation.[3]

Guides combine experience with social and emotional skills to determine which leadership style is most appropriate for their groups and current conditions. Expert guides toggle smoothly through leadership styles in a process that Exum guide and two-time world extreme ski champion Doug Coombs called "educational guiding," or simply, "teach, coach, guide." Doug, who took clients steep skiing and ski mountaineering on the most challenging of slopes and couloirs around the world, told me that he that would *teach* by giving clients little drills and techniques to help them ski through tough terrain; *coach* by actually showing them the way and how to do it; and *guide* firmly, requiring compliance, if conditions on the mountain were uncertain or changing for the worse.

Coombs said:

> Guiding in the most challenging conditions becomes "I need you to do what I say. Right now we are not teaching and we are not coaching. You are following directions while I get us through the situation that's at hand." As a guide I want the client to be absolutely safe. Most of the time, people perform at their highest levels when they are most confident, and when they are most confident they are happy and they're going to try hard. If you are going to instill confidence in clients through being light-hearted, then you also have to tell them there will be a time when seriousness is needed. That's when we have to focus.

Feña Yañez, a Vertical guide experienced in guiding trekking expeditions in Antarctica, uses several leadership styles during the day:

> There are three decisive moments. At the start, we discuss what we are doing that day, sharing what the team needs to know on this leg of the trek, so they can see me as a resource actively working with them. During the day most people will see me as hands off, but what I am really doing is working with the trek's leader of the day. He or she has my full attention. If I need to speak with that person, I avoid doing it at the front of the group. I will coach them to work more closely with their navigator, and if there's a junior guide assigned to me, I will work with them too, to try to help them see things through my eyes. All the same, if there's something that needs to be addressed, a good teaching moment, we will just stop and have a discussion. I find that if you stop during the day and do mini-debriefs, the conversation is a lot easier at night. You can say, "Remember what happened at Stop 1 and Stop 2?" Finally, when it's time for the evening meeting, I will help a team member take the lead on facilitating a discussion, as the team talks through what happened that day. But there are two scenarios in which you need to be directive: emergencies and safety calls. If I need to intervene with a rope team moving on delicate and exposed terrain in Antarctica, it can be two minutes of being a sergeant—but then it's over.

Participant Reflections

- Most people associate leadership with giving orders, but going on the trip made me appreciate the aspect of leadership that most people take for granted—mentoring. Aptly called *guides*, they showed us how to scale our personal summits by sharing their collective wisdom and experience with us climbers. When they warned us about past mistakes they had made on the trail—stepping on the rope, standing too close to the edge of the cliff—we learned to avoid those traps and watch out for the safety of the whole group. Moreover, they knew when to allow us to collect our own battle scars, thus making the lessons stick. Instead of holding my hand every step of the way, for instance, the guides let me slip in order to stand. They made me scale walls one-handed and then eventually no-handed, until I was comfortable enough to trust that my sticky shoes would cling to the rocks. *(Grand Teton Mountaineering)*

- Our second day of climbing school involved smaller teams, new guides and more difficult pitches. We attacked the rocks with both a greater sense of excitement and an understanding of the danger. My guide was friendly, patient, and competent. She instructed us on the methodology of climbing and the responsibilities we'd face on the rocks. Unfortunately, I lost focus and failed to fulfill all my responsibilities. As the final climber on our rope, it was my job to collect the anchors and other equipment as I passed. After we completed our climb, the guide noticed immediately that I was not carrying all the equipment. She was forced to solo back through the route, picking up what I had left behind. Her reaction was not angry or spiteful. She explained how vital it is to pay attention to all our responsibilities. On a longer climb, she noted, we would have been unable to continue without the forgotten anchors and might have been stranded halfway up the slope. The equipment was also her personal property, items she had selected and purchased. She remained serious and pointed in her commentary long enough to notice that I had taken her words to heart. During the remainder of the climb, our guide waved off any discussion of the incident, returning to her earlier light-mannered and friendly attitude. Leaders are responsible for the actions of their teams. They must always be watching for signs of danger and be ready and willing to address the mistakes of their teammates. *(Grand Teton Mountaineering)*

- I found that quick decision making and adapting to new situations were critical during the trip. From my own experience and from observing others, the leaders of the day needed to make judgment calls, such as which path to take or what tasks needed to be done first at camp, to keep the day moving and guide the other group members. Furthermore, as no participant had extensive experience prior to this venture, a key component of being a leader was making decisions with limited knowledge and trusting one's own judgment. When I was leading the group as leader of the day, the others behind me depended on me to know where to go. I had to push away any uncertainties and become more confident as someone others could turn to. *(Utah)*

Exum's Al Read puts it this way:

When you're approaching the beginning of the climb, you're thinking to yourself, "OK, where am I going to put these clients?" You have to put the weakest client right behind you, put someone stronger at the number three position on the rope who will be doing most of the belaying, and someone at the end who you don't have to pay attention to. Then you start the climb. You watch everybody belay at the first pitch and you have to be very aware. The climbing isn't the hard part: the belaying is the hard part. You need to be aware of what the client is doing all the time. You have to take charge, but not in a military way, unless things get really tough, or if people get frightened or a storm comes in. You have to be firm, take charge in a nice way, but clients have to have confidence in you, so you have to show yourself as leading, put yourself in that position and hold yourself to it.

Vertical's Willie Parra agrees:

I like to help people as much as I can, so they can get to the high point or fulfill what they came for. I like to go with the slowest people, find the pace that's good for them. But sometimes you just have to give orders. Normally it happens when the conditions get rough and the client isn't feeling that good. They know they are at risk, so I make the decisions. I prefer to be clear but friendly, direct, not make the client feel bad. Sometimes it's just not the right time for you.

In an interview with Rodrigo Jordan, Mike Useem tells how Jordan adopted a surprisingly collaborative leadership style during an expedition on Lhotse, the fourth-highest mountain in the world. Useem writes:

The mountaineering tradition has long defined climbing success as the placement of at least one or two members of an expedition on the summit, with others playing essential roles of support but all enjoying the accolades of success. For its many benefits, however, that tradition always came with a price, borne by those who did not stand on the summit but who might have done so were it not for the luck of the draw or the obligation of support. That custom, however, gave way to a new concept during a breakthrough discussion led by Jordan at a base camp several years earlier. He was then leading a Chilean expedition to climb Lhotse, a 27,940-foot peak attached to Mount Everest, and his team was preparing to send a small summit team to the top of Lhotse. Jordan faced one of an expedition leader's most excruciating decisions. Many of the team's members are typically capable of reaching the summit, all have shouldered great risk in carrying supplies, and yet only a pair or two are normally accorded a chance to stand on the shoulders of others to make a final push for the top.

Jordan's climbers had assembled in a base camp tent to learn whom he would designate for the honor of the summit team. But he surprised them all by proposing to follow a very different pathway. Instead of the leader solely choosing, all of the climbers would collectively decide on the summit party, bringing far more data to bear on a critical decision since each member would contribute his own direct knowledge of the relative capabilities of all the others.

One of the climbers in the base camp tent, Kiko Guzman, proposed instead an even more novel approach: "Why not plan for all to go to the summit?" The light bulb lit, Jordan instinctively responded, "Why not?" and in an instant Jordan and his team embraced a complete break with convention. That required quick revision of a host of logistical plans: The high camp on Lhotse, for instance, barely had room for several climbers, let alone all. But just five days later, Jordan and 14 others stood on the summit of Lhotse—the first Chileans to reach the top, and all of the Chileans on the expedition.[4]

Participant Reflections

- The first thing I learned was "guide's pace." The guide explained to me that the goal of leading the group was not to speedily navigate the terrain and then stop and wait for the rest of the group, but to go slowly and deliberately, making sure everyone was comfortable with the pace. Additionally, he was always looking back to check on the group, to see how far they were behind, as well as to see if anyone was having trouble. I believe most of the guide's actions can be embodied by the phrase "Service above self." This is the motto of Rotary International, and an ideology I'd learned and forgotten over the years. *(Utah)*

- This experience has given me insight into the dynamics of leadership, especially after witnessing how our mountain guides were successful at motivating and facilitating the strenuous journey. The guide led the group by setting a steady pace. In the beginning, I watched his every step so I could copy exactly which rocks he stepped on in rhythm. As I got more comfortable and accustomed to the movement, I was able to figure out the path I wanted to take by calculating the relative heights and distances of steps, while still maintaining the group tempo. I believe that this translates to leadership universally, where the leader must first take charge and set a pace, but also allow for the individual challenge of calculation and improvisation. This made me feel comfortable and confident in the work, which resulted in a truly satisfying sense of accomplishment. I believe that a true leader's presence and encouragement should always be felt, while still leaving room for independence in carrying out tasks. This way, an individual feels responsible for his/her work and its significance, but also knows that it is part of the team effort. *(Peru)*

- The three most important lessons I learned as a leader in the wilderness were to have a plan and a backup plan; always give support to the weakest team member; and use a positive attitude to motivate the group These lessons were put to the test when it was my responsibility to guide the group through a difficult kayak portage. We were accompanied on this trip by four experienced guides, but through the most strenuous part of the portage their attention was diverted by the loss of three kayaks down a series of dangerous rapids. This left it to me to keep the group moving and safely transport the kayaks over a cliff edge to the other side of the lake. The most valuable lesson from the guides that I put to use was the importance of attitude in motivating the group. I cannot claim to be the most experienced leader nor physically the strongest member of the team, but that day I was the most upbeat. I made it my responsibility to fill the silence with bad jokes, funny stories, and cheers of encouragement for team members. Using overwhelmingly positive energy to take their minds off the physically grueling task at hand kept the momentum going forward. Even if my own body was feeling the strain of exhaustion, the most important contribution I could make would be to set a positive example. *(Patagonia)*

Does a Leader Need to Be Extroverted?

Professors Deniz S. Ones and Stephan Dilchert reported in a 2009 study that while just 50 percent of the general population is extroverted, some 96 percent of managers and executives display extroverted personalities: their research shows that the proportion of highly extroverted managers and executives increases steadily at each level in the management hierarchy, from 30 percent of supervisors to 41 percent of middle managers to 60 percent of top executives.[5] Adam Grant, Francesca Gino, and David Hofmann, writing in the *Harvard Business Review*, say extroverts are favored in hiring and promotion decisions, and are perceived to be more effective by supervisors and subordinates alike: other research shows that 65 percent of senior corporate executives viewed introversion as a barrier to leadership and that highly extroverted U.S. presidents are perceived as more effective.[6]

From these findings one might imagine that all successful leaders must have big, extroverted personalities—something that's often reinforced in the popular literature—but this certainly isn't always the case in real life. Findings from recent research on the impact of extroverted and introverted leadership styles on group performance support the need for a flexible leadership style aligned with a keen awareness of followers' preferences. Management professor Adam Grant and co-authors, writing in the *European Business Review*, acknowledge that extroverted individuals are more likely to seek out and rise into leadership positions. But, Grant and coauthors ask, is it possible that extroverted leaders are not always effective? While extroverted leaders bring the vision, assertiveness and energy necessary to give direction, they also tend to "seek out and command the spotlight."[7] In fact, Susan Cain, author of *Quiet*, writes, "We tend to overestimate how outgoing leaders need to be."[8]

Elizabeth Bernstein, writing in the *Wall Street Journal*, says that extroverts gain energy from being with other people and typically process information externally, preferring to talk through problems, forming opinions as they speak. Introverts, meanwhile, feel at their most alive and most energized in quieter situations and process information internally. The idea that entrepreneurs must be gregarious and commanding, "verbally adept and able to inspire employees, clients, and investors with the sheer force of their personality," simply doesn't match reality. Now, Bernstein reports, business experts and psychologists say describing entrepreneurs as extroverts disregards the unique skills that introverts bring to the workplace, including "the ability to focus for long periods, a propensity for balanced and critical thinking, and a knack for quietly empowering others." Bernstein identifies a number of well-known entrepreneurs who are either self-identified introverts or who have many introvert qualities, including Bill Gates of Microsoft, Steve Wozniak of Apple, Larry Page of Google—and even Warren Buffett, chairman and CEO of Berkshire Hathaway.[9]

Participant Reflections

- An optimistic, positive attitude is crucial to maintaining a team's morale. A leader's spirit quite often reflects the mental state of the entire team. If he/she becomes despondent in the face of an immediate obstacle, the team will have very little chance of overcoming it. Thus, the leader should always look for hope when judging a situation. *(Utah)*

- Each guide had a unique style of leadership. One used expectations to motivate the group. His own zest inspired us, and made us want to complete the challenges because we knew he expected nothing less. The other relied more on support to motivate the group. She remained positive throughout all of the physical challenges, simply smiling and offering encouraging words. Her own calmness and positivity washed over the group and kept morale high. *(Iceland)*

- On days when plans had to change, the guides did this with such ease that it was hardly evident there was a change in schedule at all. This impressed me so much because I am aware of how easy it can be to get caught up when a day or event doesn't go exactly according to schedule. I learned an important lesson in leadership here: remaining calm and spending time looking for an alternative, rather than thinking about what could have been, is the most effective way to approach the situation. *(Iceland)*

- From a management perspective, I think that guides are the perfect example of leading from within a group. They take the time to get to know all of the members of the trip and work to join our group as fluidly as possible. Most importantly, having taken the time to learn about each person's personal and physical capabilities, they do an incredible job of offering help when it is needed and stepping back when they know you can finish a task. Essentially, the guides walk the very fine line of doing too much or too little very well. *(Peru)*

Grant and his coauthors' workplace findings also reveal that leadership style can enhance or inhibit team performance depending on the level of proactivity of team members. Their study confirms that the best outcomes are achieved when extroverted leaders are matched with more passive followers and introverted leaders with more proactive followers. Research suggests that extroverted leaders are more likely to be threatened by proactive followers who might "steal the spotlight" and challenge the leader's dominance, authority, and status; introverted leaders are more willing to consider and use input from outspoken team members. When proactivity from team members is needed, Grant suggests, it may be wise for extroverted leaders to step out of the spotlight and move to a more supportive and encouraging style of leading.[10]

From Doug Coombs's flexible "teach, coach, guide" model of guiding, to Goleman's work on leadership styles, to Grant's findings on the impact of extroverted and introverted leadership styles on group performance, the best guides know intuitively that in their dynamic and highly uncertain environments, there is a place for a wide range of leadership styles. A skilled guide makes it all work seamlessly by assessing conditions and the environment as well as the competence and disposition of their clients, and applying the right leadership style at the right time.

In Practice

Seychelle Hicks, who participated in multiple guided expeditions on the Grand Teton and in Patagonia and later in Antarctica and the Himalayas, is a customer success manager lead at BloomReach, a big-data digital-marketing startup in Silicon Valley. She was formerly an M&A associate in investment banking in New York City. She writes:

> While a guide is typically envisioned as climbing at the "sharp end" of the rope, breaking trail, or setting the pace, I have found that the best guides not only have extraordinary physical endurance, technical aptitude, and tenacious drive, but also demonstrate the ability to quickly and effectively adapt their leadership style to the changing conditions on the mountain.
>
> While trekking up to the Lower Saddle of the Grand Teton, I observed guide Christian Santelices effortlessly and swiftly dancing across the rocks as he worked his way up the steep terrain. How did he do it with such ease, when my calves were starting to tighten so early in the day? Christian noticed me stretching my calves at a rest point and quietly approached in his usual soft-spoken way to recommend that I search for features on the trail—a rock, a root, a groove—to bring my heel into a more parallel plane with my forefoot, which would help to recruit my stronger, larger quadriceps muscles.
>
> The seemingly simple task to put one foot in front of the other was now no longer laborious, but became a fun game of trial and error to learn the "mountain step." As we neared our camp, I accidentally dislodged some small rocks, which tumbled down the trail. Christian instantly heard the rocks come loose, despite being quite some distance below on the trail, and immediately yelled "ROCK!" to alert the rest of the team. Fortunately no one was injured by my misstep. While at one moment Christian was fully alert and ready to warn the team, in the same breath he was quick to regain his calm demeanor and continue quietly up the trail.
>
> During these brief but personally impactful events, Christian displayed multiple leadership styles—leading by example, demonstrating mountaineering expertise, coaching me to use a more effective step, and encouraging my progress, while also providing constructive feedback.
>
> In my role at BloomReach, I am responsible for my team delivering results to our customers, driving company revenue, and executing projects across multiple cross-functional teams. As a team manager and individual contributor, I am required to adapt throughout the day to our customers, resourcing

demands and building an effective and self-directed team to navigate the fast-paced world of a growing and scaling company.

In each of my actions, I strive to best suit the needs of the situation by picking up small nuances and cues, just as Christian did on the Grand Teton. Like a guide whose experience shows in each step they take, I rely on my reputation and credibility to lead by example and to set the tone of the team. To encourage ownership and self-direction, I create a list of key points during customer meetings or projects to provide specific and timely feedback, and challenge our team to propose and try new solutions. I try to strike the right balance of only jumping in when needed—like to call an alert for a "ROCK!"

The Message

Learn the ropes from guides who have developed their leadership styles working with clients of all levels on the world's toughest mountains. Doug Coombs practiced his "teach, coach, guide" method on the steepest of snow slopes, aligning his style with the skill level of his clients and the terrain they were traversing. Guides are adept at coaching and supporting their clients during their adventures, yet none are shy about providing clear direction when conditions call for it. Susan Cain, and Adam Grant and his co-authors, helpfully point out the unique leadership strengths of those who are more introverted, while Elizabeth Bernstein identifies a few spectacularly successful leaders with a preference for this style. Daniel Goleman's research has found that some managers' leadership styles have a positive impact on organizational climate, while others can have a negative impact over time. Read more about building effective leadership styles in the action steps to follow.

ACTION STEPS FOR BUILDING EFFECTIVE LEADERSHIP STYLES

Kevin Sharer, former CEO of pioneering biotechnology firm Amgen, says that when the fast growth of his company pressured it to develop the talent already in its leadership pipeline, the top management team put the focus on the behaviors executives were expected to display. Amgen came up with a set of expectations for leaders: consciously act as a role model; deliver strong results in the right way; build, develop, and lead empowered and diverse teams; and motivate others with a vision for the future that can be implemented. Putting the focus on the behaviors of company leaders, Sharer says, opens the door to a valuable diversity of leadership style differences, and doing so encourages vigorous internal discussion of the behaviors leaders expect of themselves and others—and on which they will be evaluated. Moreover, suggests Sharer, a focus on behavior underscores two key messages: "It isn't worth much to have an attribute that you don't display; and, if you fall short of what the best leaders do, you can close that gap."[11]

Consider these action steps to help you build effective leadership styles:

- **Engage your organization in a discussion of expected leader behaviors—and then enforce them.**
  - Amgen senior executives did the hard work themselves. They carefully considered a set of behaviors they expected of leaders and then presented the findings to their top 100 people, asking them to push back on language and even add new items. Once the process was completed, Amgen fostered the behaviors through evaluations, surveys, and communications—and through the very visible actions of their executives. To put teeth into it, consistent and significant violations could result in dismissal.[12]

- **Build strengths in a variety of leadership styles—and know when to use them.**
  - Drawing on a random sample of almost 4,000 executives selected from a database of more than 20,000 executives worldwide, Daniel Goleman identified six key leadership styles—*coercive, authoritative, affiliative, democratic, pacesetting,* and *coaching*—that leaders can strategically use to enhance performance. According to Goleman, "coercive leaders demand immediate compliance, authoritative leaders mobilize people toward a vision, affiliative leaders create emotional bonds and harmony, democratic leaders build consensus through participation, pacesetting leaders expect excellence and self-direction, and coaching leaders develop people for the future." Goleman explains how each style has its roots in emotional intelligence, in what kinds of situations each is most effective, and whether the overall effect of a given style is positively or negatively correlated with organizational climate. His conclusion: The most effective leaders use a collection of leadership styles, and are able to flexibly match their choice of leadership style to the situation. Further, the authoritative, affiliative, democratic, and coaching styles (in decreasing order) are positively correlated with the best working atmosphere. While there is a short-term place for the coercive and pacesetting styles in organizations—Goldman says a coercive style can be entirely appropriate during a true emergency, and a pacesetting style can work well for leaders of skilled workers who are intrinsically motivated—their overall impact on climate is negative.[13]

- **Match your leadership style to the changing view of what a leader does.**
  - What Peter Senge, a pioneer of systems thinking, wrote in 1990 still rings very true today: "Our traditional view of leaders—as special people who set the direction, make decisions, and energize the troops—is deeply rooted in an individualistic and nonsystemic worldview. Especially in the West, leaders are heroes—great men (and occasionally women) who rise to the fore in times of crisis. So long as such myths prevail, they reinforce a focus on short-term events and charismatic heroes rather than on systemic forces and collective learning." Senge proposes that, for organizations that want to continuously learn and grow, the leader's role will differ from that of the charismatic decision maker. Consider, then, what leadership styles you might want to use if you were to lead, as Senge suggests, as a designer, teacher, and

steward of the organization, "building organizations where people are continually expanding their capabilities to shape their future . . ."[14] Read Senge's
seminal paper, then revisit Goleman's six leadership styles to see which styles
you think might work best in your own learning organization.

- **Create a sense of psychological safety in teams by encouraging risk-taking
  without fear of punishment.**
  - Adam Grant, Wharton management professor and author of the bestselling
    book *Give and Take*, attributes the success of Emmy Award–winning com-
    edy writer George Meyer (*Saturday Night Live, The Simpsons*) to his stance
    as a "giver" (helping others without expecting anything in return) and to the
    way he chose to work with others—freely collaborating with and supporting
    his colleagues and generously offering feedback. Grant quotes Meyer as say-
    ing, "I tried to create a climate in the room where everybody feels that they
    can contribute, that it's okay to fall on your face many, many times."[15] Har-
    vard researcher Amy Edmondson demonstrated that team leader coaching
    and support were important contributors to building an atmosphere of psy-
    chological safety that would facilitate team learning. "The need for learning
    in work teams is likely to become increasingly critical as organizational
    change and complexity intensify," Edmondson writes. Successful teams need
    to be able to "ask questions, seek help, and tolerate mistakes in the face of
    uncertainty—while team members and other colleagues watch . . ."[16]

- **Lead like a guide—or a gardener.**
  - General Stanley McChrystal's last assignment was to command all Ameri-
    can and coalition forces in Afghanistan (Joint Special Operations Task
    Force). His experience commanding the task force in an era of rapidly chang-
    ing warfare tactics led him to discard conventional wisdom and redesign
    both the task force structure and how it was led. McChrystal, echoing Senge,
    says we still tend to gravitate toward heroic leaders who lead by "crafting bril-
    liant strategies and distributing precise commands." But, according to
    McChrystal, "the organization as a rigidly reductionist mechanical beast is
    an endangered species. The speed and interconnected nature of the new
    world in which we function have rendered it too stupid and slow to survive
    the onslaught of predators. . . . it simply lumbers into tar pits, lacks the
    strength to free itself, and slowly dies." The traditional, all-knowing heroic
    leader, he says, may not be far behind. In McChrystal's fast-moving and
    interconnected world of special operations, the senior leadership role that
    emerged instead was one of "an empathetic crafter of culture." McChrystal
    realized that his new leadership role had to shift from all-knowing to "tend-
    ing the garden," shaping the culture by leading through example and mes-
    sage, and providing room for input from a widely distributed staff. His daily
    operations and intelligence video teleconference with key personnel at more
    than 70 locations became his opportunity to demonstrate his commitment
    to being seen live as a commander, and, at the same time, to provide the

chance for more junior officers to step up and speak, and to receive helpful feedback. "Thank you," McChrystal says, became his most important phrase, and "interest and enthusiasm my most powerful behaviors." The message, in terms of leadership style is pretty clear: "Gardeners plant and harvest, but more than anything, they *tend*."[17]

SEVEN

Guides Empower Others to Reach Their Own Summits

Providing the space for growth and development

Empowerment is not about giving people new authority and new responsibilities and then walking away. It is all about removing barriers.
—DAN COHEN and JOHN KOTTER

True leadership is about consistently striving to lift others up.
—EXPEDITION PARTICIPANT

Yang Sun's climb on the Grand Teton required guide Christian Santelices to balance the concerns of fellow guide Amy Carse with Sun's strong desire to reach for the summit. Santelices agreed with Carse's stand on safety for the climbing team, but he also understood his client's need to reach as high as she possibly could. One of the key leadership strengths of guides is the ability to identify and build on a client's strengths, and to provide the space for growth and development, even under challenging conditions. Santelices proposed a workable alternative that eventually empowered Yang Sun to reach her own summit while deftly balancing Carse's concern for safety for her team. "It was Yang's journey," Santelices said, "and it was her summit. It was my job to help her reach her own outcome."

Increasing one's feelings of self-efficacy and control and removing conditions that foster a sense of powerlessness has been popularly referred to as empowerment. Empowering leaders delegate authority, involve others in making decisions, engage in consultative behaviors, and use others' ideas and suggestions. Professor Shahidul Hassan and co-authors say that such behavior signals a leader's confidence and trust.[1] Research conducted by Josh Arnold and his study team revealed that critical leader behaviors in empowered team environments in three diverse industries included leading by example, coaching, participative decision making, informing, and showing concern/interacting with the team. These behaviors (with an emphasis on developing others and influencing commitment) characterize "leadership" rather than "management" behaviors.[2]

Exum guide Jim Williams says:

> If you want to get to the summit of the Grand Teton or Mount Everest, my job as a guide is to provide you with a shoulder to stand on so you can get to the summit, not for me to give you a hand up *from* the summit so you can join me on something. From my perspective, it's not about me reaching the summit, but it's for you to do that and for me to be the vehicle, or to be part of that process so that you are able to step further into the things that you are less comfortable with, to reduce the risk to a level that you're comfortable with so you can continue. Creating the environment that allows a climber to do their best and perform at the highest level possible is the ultimate measure of success as a guide in the mountains . . . the guide and clients should strive to reach this new height. . . . if the summit is part of this achievement, then great, but this alone is success.

Participant Reflections

- The guides walked the perfect balance between leading by example and allowing us to grow on our own. Our personal development was obviously their top priority. At the beginning of every day, they asked us to outline our goals, and equipped us with the skills necessary to achieve those milestones. They then allowed us to continue the cycle by instructing others and helping them achieve their own goals in the process. (*Grand Teton Mountaineering*)

- The technical skill and expertise of the guides no doubt increased our confidence greatly. They led quietly, blending into the background when they could and allowed others to take the lead. They served as mentors and made sure that everyone was safe and sound, but did not crave the limelight. *(Grand Teton Mountaineering)*

- I learned that I shouldn't be afraid to step off the beaten path and try things a different way. The guides are certainly present to lead, but this doesn't mean that you have to follow in their exact footsteps. Often, they can make sure that another path or activity is safe, even if the entire group doesn't engage in it. I discovered this on the first day of our venture, when the guide and I were at the front of the line. He turned to me and asked if I wanted to go to the top of a hill that we were originally going to go around. The entire group ended up following us, and we had a spectacular view of the surrounding landscape as well as a nice bed of moss to eat lunch on and take a nap. But I wanted to take it a step further. I asked the guide if I could climb up to the peak of the mountain that we were on, and he said I could go on my own. At the top I could see for miles, and even though I was alone, it was one of my favorite moments of the trip. Although guidance was necessary to complete the trip, it didn't stop me from taking the initiative and making my own discoveries. From a leadership perspective, this experience also taught me that you must be willing to let those under your direction take their own approach and try new things. This will result in a much richer experience for both individuals and the entire team. *(Iceland)*

Vertical guide Gabriel Becker agrees:

What makes me love what I do is to give another person the option to experience something that will change and move them to see something they never expected to find again. People need to believe in themselves and learn new things about themselves. A trek in Bhutan can take a participant to over 16,000 feet and require them to walk eight hours a day. When they are confronted by this, and find they can do it, that is so empowering.

Becker's colleague, Kiko Guzman, adds, "When you guide a client you have a chance to teach not only technical skills, but also the chance to teach how you see life. People who hire you are looking for something different in life, and they are very open to learn and grow—it's easy to teach a person who is open in this way."

Guides, in fact, are the ultimate "givers," to use a term that management professor Adam Grant has coined to describe successful people who contribute value without worrying about what they receive in return.[3] Guides coach their clients continuously and generously, always working to empower their charges to reach as high as they can.

Exum's Jack Turner says:

The first thing I would want for a client is a full understanding that they can do more than they think they can. It's the primary lesson of climbing. I think one of the best things we can do, in terms of instruction or guiding, is to give people a sense of competence or trust in their body, or as I like to say, "The world's a dangerous place and you're OK!" You can master the skills to wander around in this dangerous environment and be fine.

Amy Carse adds, "It's so inspiring to guide first-timers. They try so hard, it makes me want to try harder in my own climbing. They want to try something new, a goal. They need something that is exciting and challenging, against all the norms of their family." Jack Tackle agrees: "It's about learning and facilitating self-discovery. I'm putting a client in an environment of personal growth that can happen only through experience. I push them to do something they wouldn't do on their own. Right at their limit, but still within the realms of safety and possibility, and they can learn from it."

Participant Reflections

- I realize that the primary purpose of the venture consisted of developing individual leadership skills and abilities within a team setting. Personally, the main lesson I gained from this venture was to take the time to look back and help the people behind you, rather than solely focusing on advancing forward. As we headed up Dead Woman's Pass, I became the person falling behind, and the day's trek leaders made the effort to ensure that I drank enough water, ate enough food, and carried a reasonable weight in my backpack. Leaders are in charge of ensuring the entire group succeeds, and this not only consists of making sure the people in the front keep moving forward, but also checking on the people that fall behind and helping them move forward as well. *(Peru)*

- Our guide allowed every participant to grow individually but was always there when we needed advice or guidance. He recognized our want to experiment and try things out on our own. By not forcing us to do things a certain way, I trusted that he had my best interests at heart and that, if I needed to, I could go to him with any questions or concerns I had without hesitation. He showed that being a successful leader does not require directing others or taking part in every minute detail, but rather simply being aware of others and their actions. *(Utah)*

- As the venture progressed, our guide became more and more hands-off. This was not because he became separated from the group, but instead because as he taught us new leadership and outdoor skills he wanted us to demonstrate our strengths and weaknesses to each other. He was always at hand and had no problem stepping in if necessary. The leader must first take charge and set a pace, but also allow for the individual challenge of calculation and improvisation. He took care never to chastise an individual in front of the group and would work one-on-one with anyone who needed assistance. This allowed each of us to hone our individual skills while also building cohesiveness and trust throughout the group. We all could clearly see each other's value to the group as a whole and were able to work together as a successful team by the end of the trip. *(Patagonia)*

The logic of empowerment is well supported by research. Management professor Natalia Lorinkova and her co-authors compared two styles of leadership: directive and empowering. A directive leadership approach focuses on providing detailed instructions, and making decisions with limited subordinate input. Being directive, they found, may make a group's initial accomplishment of tasks easier by providing explicit instructions and focusing efforts toward individual tasks, reducing ambiguity, and establishing clear rules for behavior. Empowering leadership, on the other hand, enhances creativity through its effects on psychological empowerment, intrinsic motivation, and engagement in the process. Lorinkova's study revealed that although teams participating in an experiment led by directive leaders started performing well more *quickly* than teams given more freedom and opportunity for input, their performance plateaued as the experiment progressed. Empowered teams, on the other hand, improved over time, eventually outstripping the performance of the directed group. The improved performance of the empowered teams was attributed in part to enhanced opportunities for team learning, behavioral coordination, and the development of collective knowledge structures.[4]

Empowering guides lead by example (guides model behavior), coach towards self-reliance (guides coach before and throughout the process), ask for team input (guides ask clients about their comfort level with the climb or trek), keep them informed (on weather conditions and route), and show concern for the entire climbing party (by building caring and supportive personal relationships). Exum's longtime practice of requiring novice clients to complete a structured training program before a summit attempt, or checking out more experienced climbers on a challenging pitch or two before setting out on a long climb, is routine practice for all of their guides. During the training program, guides ask each climber to build and demonstrate some key skills on which others' lives will depend, enhancing feelings of self-efficacy. Clients gradually become self-reliant in belaying and rope management, and guides coach, encourage, and support them throughout the process. Similarly, Vertical's practice of requiring clients who want to climb big Himalayan peaks to train with them over an extended period indicates the same concern for the client's growth and development.

Exum's Mark Newcomb says:

> In climbing you have this very clear goal to get to the top and you can't do that unless you bring out the strengths of people and put them to use in the team to reach the goal. You need to place them in the right position to help the flow, and shift roles or positions to keep the flow going. The goal has to be a worthy one. Once I see that someone has a strength and is using it, I will back off. It's great to let someone go. I see them thinking, "Let's see, what do I need to do now?" Suddenly the light bulb goes on, and they've got it, they're good to go. Otherwise, you're constantly grabbing the rope, telling them what to do.

With a successful and supportive basic training program, and an accurate assessment, guides help the client reach as high on the mountain as they are able, sometimes higher than the client ever imagined was possible. Guides, however, also maintain a fine line between assuring climbers that they can overcome adversity, and telling them in just the right way if they sense that the climber is exhausted or the risk too great, that the summit is out of reach on this ascent.

Participant Reflections

- I once had a teacher who always used to tell her students, "I respect your intelligence." She would repeat it so much that we were soon no longer in doubt of our intelligence. Her intent was to remind us that even though she may be far more knowledgeable, she had a responsibility to learn from us just as much as we did from her and, moreover, that we had a certain responsibility to own our intelligence. In Iceland, our guides were the teachers, who, through their patient and trusting guidance, seemed to continually say, "I respect your strength." Throughout the entire trip they planted a belief in our hearts that we would be capable of trekking long distances and summiting any number of glaciers, however high they may be. From the beginning they walked with us, slid down snowy slopes, sloshed through frigid waters, and felt the rain on their faces as we inched toward hazy horizons. They believed in us, so we believed in ourselves. *(Iceland)*

- True leadership is about consistently striving to lift others up. Although no one was preaching to us about how to be a leader or how we needed to behave, the guides displayed seemingly effortless leadership simply by leading by example. It became clear to me that the key to leading by example is to work selflessly for others, rather than focusing on getting to your final destination as quickly as possible. Although our guides were extremely experienced climbers and strong athletes, they consistently praised us for our hard work and humble hiking abilities. They spoke genuinely and made me feel truly accomplished for my work, even though they each could have completed our entire trek in virtually half the time. Rather than showing off their great skills, their humility and strength allowed them to shine as leaders, even when waiting for the slowest hiker to reach the summit. *(Peru)*

- A good leader is clear about what she expects, but then trusts her followers to live up to those goals. If you give those you are leading room to be creative and pursue their own ideas, often you will be surprised at how much they can accomplish. *(Iceland)*

Exum's Christian Santelices says:

You really are building others up, inspiring clients to find in themselves what they might not have thought themselves capable of. Anybody who comes and wants to climb the mountain has to think that they can make it. Yes, occasionally a guide has to turn a client back from the summit. Sometimes it's simply "You're right, today's not the day." But more likely it's "If you push just a little bit, right here, you're going to make it through this, one step at a time. You can do it."

In Practice

Edmund Reese, vice president and chief financial officer for U.S. consumer card products at American Express, climbed the Grand Teton as a member of a guide-led team. Several years after his climb with our team, I ran into him again at the Wharton School, where he was completing the executive MBA program. Thinking back on what he learned from his experience, Reese told me:

> Having leadership responsibility for over 2,000 people, I've learned that to achieve our objectives and enjoy the work on the way to success, I must take the first big step. Like our guides on the Grand, I've focused on formulating a clear communication for all members and articulating a vision. That helps the group clear the mind of clutter and focus. The guides also instilled a confidence in me from the moment of our first encounter. There was no doubt in my mind that under their guidance we would indeed reach the peak. Generating confidence in the workplace to ensure that members know success is attainable and there will likely be a solution for challenges has been an important focus. The leadership lessons taught both by the guides and the mountain itself has honed my focus on embracing the front lines. After the strategy is set, delegate authority and stay close to those most directly engaged with the work. If we build leadership in others, we develop a stronger line and an overall stronger organization. This approach has helped us take very bold steps and reach many objectives.

The Message

Guides work hard to create the space for their clients to accomplish what at first seems impossible. Climbing the Grand Teton—or embarking on a trek in an entirely new and remote location—can be an overwhelming experience. For a novice climber, just looking up at the massive scale of the rocks ahead (and the exposure, with drops of several thousand feet immediately below) is an intimidating, yet frequently life-changing, prospect for most beginners. And it is in this environment that guides shine, for their focus is solely on the client. Guides *lift their charges up*—spiritually and emotionally—and encourage them to climb on. In the following pages you will find some action steps for empowering those you may work with.

ACTION STEPS FOR BUILDING EMPOWERMENT

Researchers Robert Quinn and Gretchen Spreitzer discovered that *empowerment* can mean different things to different people. Quinn and Spreitzer asked a group of senior executives to define empowerment. Half said empowerment was a top-down process centering on delegation within a set of clear boundaries and holding people accountable for results. The other half saw it quite differently: they believed it meant removing barriers, trusting people, and tolerating their imperfections.[5]

In 2007, Spreitzer, a management professor at the University of Michigan, looked back at 20 years of research on empowerment, and found two complementary approaches. The *socio-structural approach* suggests that people at lower levels of the organization can be empowered if they have access to opportunity, information, support, and resources, and that this power-sharing enables workers to make decisions relevant to their own work. Spreitzer lists participative decision making, skill/knowledge-based pay, open access to information, decentralized structures, and training as some elements of this approach to empowerment. The second approach, *psychological empowerment*, moves beyond managerial practices and focuses on how employees actually experience their work. Spreitzer found that that deriving meaning from work, belief in one's competence, having a sense of self-determination or choice in work, and the extent to which a worker has impact together reflect a desirable and active orientation to one's work role.[6]

While empowerment remains a hot topic, workplace *engagement*—defined by organizational psychologists Wilmar Schaufeli and Arnold Bakker as a positive, fulfilling, work-related state of mind characterized by energy, resilience, and absorption[7]—has begun to garner just as much attention. Tony Schwartz and Christine Porath begin their 2014 *New York Times* opinion piece "Why You Hate Work" by writing:

> The way we're working isn't working. Even if you're lucky enough to have a job, you're probably not very excited to get to the office in the morning, you don't feel much appreciated while you're there, you find it difficult to get your most important work accomplished, amid all the distractions, and you don't believe that what you're doing makes much of a difference anyway. By the time you get home, you're pretty much running on empty, and yet still answering emails until you fall asleep. Increasingly, this experience is common not just to middle managers, but also to top executives.[8]

Consider these action steps to help increase a sense of empowerment and engagement:

- **Meet these four core needs in the workplace.**
  - While a 2013 study by Marcela Quiñones and co-authors in the *Journal of Work and Organizational Psychology* argues that feelings of psychological empowerment are related to higher levels of work engagement,[9] a 2013 Gallup poll, cited by Tony Schwartz and Christine Porath in their *New York Times* piece, reports that just 30 percent of employees in America feel engaged at work—and around the world the proportion of workers who say they feel engaged at work is even lower. Contributing to the problem: ever-increasing

demands on time, a leaner workforce, and a rising flood of digital informa-
tion. Employees are more likely to experience engagement at work, Schwartz
and Porath report, when these core needs are met:
- *Physical*, through opportunities to renew and recharge at work
- *Emotional*, by feeling valued and appreciated
- *Mental*, when they are able to focus on their most important tasks and
  define where and when they get their work done
- *Spiritual*, by feeling connected to a higher purpose at work[10]

- **Don't try to control people—inspire them!**
  - Bill George, former chairman and CEO of Medtronic, and now professor of
    management practice at Harvard Business School, says that if employees
    don't feel a genuine passion for their work, and believe that it makes a differ-
    ence, engagement drops off dramatically. Too many layers of management,
    and a persistent focus on short-term goals, limit creativity, while first-line
    employees face increased hours and less freedom to act. In this environment,
    George says, "desired qualities like empowerment, engagement, and inno-
    vation are subordinated to control aspects." Instead of managers who con-
    trol, George says, "we need leaders who inspire in these roles." That means
    middle managers working alongside their employees, facilitating the work
    of the people they lead by making their jobs easier, and removing bureau-
    cratic impediments and other obstacles. "All of these actions," he says, "make
    these leaders more like partners and coaches than bosses and controllers in
    the traditional sense." George offers the same advice to senior managers who
    wish to motivate and inspire workers—engage with the first line and spend
    less time in conference rooms and in one-on-one meetings.[11]

- **Empower others by doing less of what you are already good at.**
  - Herminia Ibarra, a management professor at INSEAD, says that the only way
    to become a leader is to *act* like one, which means exploring new ways to
    build and develop key leadership competencies. Relying on your current
    expertise and continuing to invest in building skills within a narrow area
    can limit your mobility within the organization, and signal a lack of leader-
    ship potential. By overinvesting in your current strengths, and microman-
    aging issues that others could handle, you can stifle your team's development.
    Her suggestions—work to become a bridge to the world outside your team,
    use what you learn to develop strategic ideas and a clear vision, engage in a
    meaningful way with people to earn their buy-in, and show through your
    actions that you walk the talk.[12]

- **Empower the capacity for leadership in others.**
  - Mike Useem, Wharton School management professor and director of Whar-
    ton's Center for Leadership and Change Management, writes, "One of the
    ironic discoveries of recent restructuring in private companies, medical cen-
    ters, and government agencies has been that giving away power judiciously
    sometimes makes one more powerful." Giving work associates more authority

to get the job done, and the tools to accomplish it, benefits both workers and managers. "A manager's ability to lead a team," Useem says, "is now a function of the team's capacity to lead as well. Spreading leadership is thus not just a matter of working down. Fostering more leadership among peers and the powers that be is a prerequisite for effectively exercising one's own. Put differently, giving away power makes one more powerful, while creating more leaders all around oneself can make one all the more a leader."[13]

- **Give empowered teams a way to signal overload conditions.**
  - MIT management professor Debora Ancona and INSEAD organizational behavior professor Henrik Bresman described an "X-team" as a team that is externally oriented, with members working effectively both inside and outside of their customary boundaries. While managing and executing within the team's boundary is necessary, it is the ability to navigate the external environment, seek out novel information, and learn and adapt that helps such teams innovate and succeed in rapidly changing environments. The researchers cite as successful examples drug development teams, product development teams, and consulting teams—all teams that face rapid change and demands for constant innovation. But what if such an empowered team begins to show signs of stress and work overload? Two key suggestions are to provide teams with a positive way to signal an unhealthy team condition by sending up a warning "flare" to senior managers, and with the freedom to communicate bad news or undue pressure that puts the work of the team at risk.[14]

- **Remove barriers.**
  - John Kotter and Dan Cohen, authors of *The Heart of Change*, write, "The word empowerment comes with so much baggage, you might be tempted to abandon it. We won't. As we use the term, empowerment is not about giving people new authority and new responsibilities and then walking away. It is all about removing barriers." Implementing a change process in an organization takes careful planning, and empowering employees is a key step.[15]
  - Some suggestions from Kotter's seminal book, *Leading Change*, include the following:
    - Ensure that employees have a shared sense of purpose.
    - Align the organizational structure with the new vision. Does the work system in place put roadblocks in the way of change?
    - Provide the training that employees need to implement change. Changing habits developed over many years takes time. Further, the new vision may call for new or unfamiliar skills, for instance, in collaboration and communication.
    - Focus on supervisors who might have their own reasons to undercut the change effort.
    - Ask whether human resource systems in place—e.g., recruiting and performance appraisal—align with the transformation effort.[16]

- **Increase engagement by highlighting the positive impact of your team's work on others.**
  - Wharton management professor Adam Grant demonstrates that one five-minute interaction with those who benefit from the organization's products and services can produce a dramatic increase in employee productivity. When customers are given an opportunity to express feedback and appreciation, in person or virtually, employees develop stronger beliefs in the impact and value of their work.[17] Two good examples from Grant's research: a brief visit from a student who had received a scholarship motivated fundraisers to increase their efforts by 400 percent, and a photograph of a patient they had never met inspired radiologists to improve the accuracy of their findings by 46 percent. Grant attributes these performance improvements to *impact* (workers see for themselves how their efforts benefit others), *appreciation* (employees feel valued by those they serve), and *empathy* (employees develop a deeper understanding of end users' problems and needs and become more committed to helping them).[18] To enhance empowerment and engagement,
    - Identify people who benefit from your team's work, including clients, customers, and suppliers—even co-workers from different divisions within your firm.
    - Arrange occasions for your team and their customers to interact and share appreciative stories, either in person or by video.
    - Meeting even a single client, customer, or end user who benefits from the team's efforts, Grant says, helps team members gain a clearer understanding of the purpose of their work, and motivates them to work "harder and smarter."
    - Ask team members to share their own stories about the difference their work has made.[19]

EIGHT

Guides Facilitate the Development of Trust

Reliability in the face of contingent outcomes

One thing we found is that it is easier to teach technical skills than to teach people how to gain trust and build teams.
—LT. GEN. WALTER F. ULMER, JR., U.S. ARMY (RET.)

I truly believe that if you cannot trust, you cannot climb.
—EXPEDITION PARTICIPANT

Thinking back to his Cerro Escudo climb, and the bonds that were established among his climbing partners and himself, Christian Santelices acknowledged that he learned a great deal about the importance of trust. He found, of course, that his partners needed him to complete the route with them, and that together they were committed to share the risk, and the rewards, of the climb. "You know, in order to get to the top," Santelices said, "I not only had to dig deep and reveal a part of my soul to the mountain, I also had to reveal a part of my soul to my partners. I learned the importance of partners, and the importance of reliance and trust. I learned about the meaning of being able to rely on those on my team—and have them rely on me."

Management professors Roger Mayer, James Davis, and David Schoorman published a widely read model of trust of one individual for another in the same year that Santelices and his partners completed their first ascent of Cerro Escudo. The need for trust, the authors say, only arises in a risky situation, for trust requires a willingness to be vulnerable to the actions of another without the ability to monitor or control that other party.[1] This was indeed the case on Cerro Escudo, in which each climber placed his life in his belay partners' hands, while fixing anchors balanced precariously many feet above.

According to Mayer and his coauthors, trust "is not taking a risk, per se, but rather it is a *willingness* to take risk"—and to put that trust to the test through action. So what causes one person to place trust in another? Three factors, Mayer and his colleagues say, are important characteristics in the person being trusted: *ability,* or special competence; *benevolence,* or the extent to which one believes another intends to do good; and *integrity*, the perception that the one being trusted adheres to an acceptable set of principles.[2]

Participant Reflections

- We were a diverse group of strangers who were able to trust each other in a few short days. This is something that some teams never achieve. I believe that it was because (and for the first time for many) there was something very real at stake: the life of a person. Each individual was accountable to the rest of the team, and a failure could result in very serious consequences. *(Grand Teton Mountaineering)*

- Although I was still continuously assessing and overcoming the risk obstacle, I found I had to focus a great deal of my thought on trust: trusting my feet, my sticky rubber shoes, the equipment, the individual belaying me, the weather, the rock, our guides, and myself. I found I could not have reservations about any of these factors, or else I simply would not get up the mountain. I truly believe that if you cannot trust, you cannot climb. It was amazing to see that when I absolutely craved overcoming the challenges set before me, I had to toss aside all inhibitions I had conjured up in my mind in the weeks and months before. If I had believed my belayer would drop me, I never would have attempted even the first pitch of basic climbing school. However, since I learned to trust literally everything around me (even to trust that a massive earthquake would probably not happen during my rappel), I was able to fully push my physical capacity and reach my goal safely. *(Grand Teton Mountaineering)*

- On the other side of trust is responsibility. When someone trusts us, we should hold ourselves accountable to them. Guide Amy Carse was right. We have the choice to say "No" when we are not ready, but when we say "Yes" we should go all out to fulfill our promises. This also relates to integrity and transparency in the business world. Leaders should always remember these responsibilities when making and announcing decisions. For example, "Climb!" *(Grand Teton Mountaineering)*

Guides deal with issues of trust on all climbs. As Rodrigo Jordan and his small team climbed the East Face of Mount Everest in 1992, he encountered a nearly vertical cleft of ice that was exposed to avalanches from above:

As I climbed the rope, using an ascender joined by a sling to my harness and a second ascender-sling to my foot, I thought about how my life was depending on a one-third-of-an-inch rope that one of my team members had anchored 130 feet above me days before. I couldn't help but ponder the profound role trust plays in mountaineering. In the many days and hours of this trip, we all had climbed together, working on this trust. This quality is such a valued asset of a team, but it requires great effort and time to build it to its utmost.[3]

Trust, to Jordan and his teammates on Everest, meant reaching for excellence in every task, including simple, everyday ones. "Whom do you trust?" Jordan asks. His answer:

The person you have seen again and again performing to his utmost capacity. Whom will I trust on the mountains? The climber I've seen checking and rechecking and checking again the batteries of his torchlight before a climb, or putting on sunscreen in the early morning. Excellence is in details. Trust is in excellence.[4]

Exum guide Jack Tackle says, "Trust is measured on past experience, on observations of making good decisions, at any given point in time having a good understanding of where the other person is. On any given day it can be different for somebody, so it's a process of observing and asking the right questions, and having good communication." Al Read adds: "Everyone has a vested interest to believe and trust that we'll be stronger together than we are alone. In climbing we depend on each other for our own safety."

When I asked Vertical guide Feña Yañez how he builds trust with clients, he told me this:

It comes by modeling what trust means to us as guides. The guides function as a team, and we model that for the rest of party. Even if it's as simple as saying, "I'll be on time," that action shows that these are our core values. On our Atacama Desert trek, there's a huge Tyrolean traverse (using a fixed line to cross from one high point to another), and you really need to trust the equipment. People think, "It is something I just can't do." At that point the guide's role is to work side by side with the client, make the experience a one-on-one thing, to connect with the person. Perhaps the extreme height has people paralyzed. If it takes all afternoon to get one person across, that's the way it is. It's never about *talking* about things, it's about *showing* them. Modeling is the key to building trust, especially if you are with people who are keen to observe.

Participant Reflections

- Over my week of mountaineering, I took the concept of trust to a different level. I defined Trust—spelled with a capital "T"—to mean that I *cannot* worry that I am unable to ensure everything is OK and according to plan. I cannot worry. There was no way I could make sure everything was all right with the person belaying me, just as there was no way for the person I was belaying to check up on me. All I could do was make sure my knot was tied correctly, make it up the pitch, and be there to ensure the safety of the climber behind me. In other words, I would do my part and the others would do theirs. I am unable to control everything. This implies a strong reliance on the group, which is a necessity in climbing. I came to see my climbing partners as an extension of myself. When the person belaying me shouted an order, I acted. When the person below me offered some guidance, I acted. This new meaning of *Trust* had many implications for me throughout the rest of the trip—it meant my life was not entirely in my hands. Within a leadership setting, there is a lot that could be gained with a shift from trust to *Trust. (Grand Teton Mountaineering)*

- The lesson that words hold weight really hit me on the second day of climbing school. At this point we were making our way up a steep cliff, with one person climbing and another person holding the rope in case the person ahead fell. The guide had moved on ahead to speed up the ascent. When it was my turn to hold that rope I knew that nothing else in the world mattered except for the person on the other end of the rope. I told him I was ready for him to climb. I knew that if I did not mean what I said, a slight slip-up could turn to tragedy. Too many times we hear people say things just to say them. Leaders must remember that people listen to what they say and that their words create expectations. If leaders do not commit to what they say and do not meet expectations, they will not command power or influence. *(Grand Teton Mountaineering)*

- When learning something for the first time, I find myself feeling inadequate if I do not immediately grasp the concepts. Because I am fearful of becoming embarrassed, rather than ask for clarification I may remain silent and hope that the pieces of the puzzle will miraculously fit together and make sense. Clearly such a stance is inefficient and wastes time and productivity, yet this trait still arises from time to time. However, in the world of mountain climbing, the guides become concerned if it appears that you understand all concepts straight away, because they know that this is seldom the case! My mindset changed quickly when I was having trouble tying a knot. What's the importance of one knot? For me, it was that this single piece of rope was the only thing standing between me and a potential drop of hundreds of feet. As such, it was not the time to pretend that when I was on the mountain my hands would take on a mind of their own and tie the knot perfectly. Rather, the training session was the time to tell the guide that I was having difficulty with this area, and ask, "Could we go over it again for clarification?" I learned that I was not the first person who had such a difficulty. It's OK to make mistakes. And it's OK if you have difficulty with something. But what's not OK is to do nothing about it. The help and resources are there, but you need to make the first move and ask that "simple" question. *(Grand Teton Mountaineering)*

Anthony Giddens, a British sociologist, tells us that there would be no need to trust anyone whose activities were continually visible and whose thought processes were transparent, or, for that matter, to trust any system whose workings were wholly known and understood. Trust, according to Giddens, means that while one party lacks full information there is also the connotation of "reliability in the face of contingent outcomes."[5] To Rodrigo Jordan, that expectation of reliability in his partners—*Excellence is in details—Trust is in excellence*—meant the difference between life and death on Mount Everest.

Trust, Giddens says, "is not the same as faith in the reliability of a person or system; it is what derives from that faith. *Trust is precisely the link between faith and confidence*"[6] (italics added). Guides know the learning process that novice climbers go through is a key part of building trust in oneself and in others: learning first to walk on smooth boulders just a few feet off the ground, practicing rope skills with new or unfamiliar partners on a grassy slope, climbing progressively more challenging pitches in teams, and taking real responsibility for each other's safety. As climbers take risks, and build faith in themselves and their climbing party, they learn to trust, and from that trust arises confidence.

In the case of trust in each other, Giddens again reminds us, the presumption of reliability involves the attribution of "probity"—seeing the highest principles, character, and integrity in others.[7] Character is rarely demonstrated more vividly than when climbers scale a rock face, linked together by a rope in a living, vital expression of trust. Guides facilitate the trust-building process from the very beginning, creating a positive learning environment by modeling behavior and providing support. Guides don't rush this process, for they know that faith, trust, and confidence come from positive experience gained over time.

The Study of Character

Anthony Giddens emphasized the importance of character and integrity to trust. The study of character occupied no less a man than Benjamin Franklin (1706–1790), who devised a "bold and arduous project of arriving at moral perfection" through which he hoped to "live without committing any fault at any time." Franklin's list of virtues, 13 in all, ranged from temperance to humility, and his aim was to acquire "the habitude of all these virtues." Accordingly, he set out to fix his attention on one virtue at a time, and when master of that, to proceed on to another, "'till I should have gone thro' the thirteen." Franklin, as was his custom, kept a detailed listing of each virtue and his progress towards the mastery of each.[8]

Between 2000 and 2003, Chris Peterson and Martin Seligman's ground-breaking research effort at the University of Pennsylvania to develop a new classification of character strengths identified six virtues—the core characteristics valued by moral philosophers and religious thinkers—and 24 character strengths that define the virtues.[9] They reviewed vast amounts of information, both historical and modern, and their research drew inspiration from written texts from ancient cultures recognized for their influential and enduring impact on human civilization, including Confucianism, Taoism, Buddhism, and Hinduism, as well as ancient Greece, Judeo-Christianity, and Islam. An important result of the research by Peterson and Seligman is the VIA Survey of Character Strengths.[10]

Mike Erwin, now CEO of the Quiet Leadership Institute, took a fresh look at the importance of character in challenging environments. Mike, who served in both Iraq and Afghanistan before his appointment as an instructor at the U.S. Military Academy at West Point, completed a graduate degree in psychology at the University of Michigan. As part of his master's thesis, he provided a list of the 24 character strengths found in the VIA survey to 42 military officers and asked them to rate how important each strength was to them in combat situations. He found that military officers in combat rated the character strengths of bravery, teamwork, perseverance, social intelligence, judgment, and honesty as the six most important to the mission of mobilizing their soldiers.

After talking with Mike during a meeting at West Point a few years ago, I recruited 36 credentialed members of the American Mountain Guide Association (AMGA), and asked them to identify the character strengths most important to their work guiding clients. I found that guides named social intelligence, leadership, appreciation of beauty and excellence, honesty, judgment, and curiosity as most important to their work. Interestingly, in addition to social intelligence and judgment, both officers in combat situations and mountain guides listed honesty as one of the top character strengths important to their work. Giddens, with his focus on "probity" in trust, would approve.

Exum's Jack Turner puts trust into perspective by harking back to the early days of big-wall climbing in California:

How is it that the early Yosemite climbers became so successful in business? There are just certain things that are crossovers from being a really good climber and being an executive. First of all, you have to take responsibility for your own decisions. Second, it requires a great deal of courage. It's not as if you have courage in just one area of your life—courage is a virtue. If you tend to have an enormous amount of courage, if you're risk-tolerant let's say, that's not only a required trait in a climber, it's also a required trait in business. Third, a climber is never alone up there, you're always part of a team. The big ascents on El Capitan were done by a small group of climbers—Royal Robbins, Yvon Chouinard, Tom Frost, and Chuck Pratt. They wouldn't go up without each other. They really believed in each other, and it was that trust in each member of the team that allowed them to get up there in situations where they couldn't easily get back down. Their trust was based in shared experience, and a strong set of similar values.

Participant Reflections

- Technical climbing demands a level of trust that will prove important in all aspects of life. When you are roped together with another climber who will be belaying you up a rock face, your life is in their hands. In climbing, just as in life, you must choose wisely those with whom you will work. You must have confidence in their reciprocal trust and capabilities. *(Grand Teton Mountaineering)*

- The Owen Chimney was the hardest pitch. It was at a point in the climb at which turning back wasn't an option and staying put wasn't a good idea. At the start of the pitch my hands were already numb and my backside was getting there. The rock was covered in verglas (a thin coating of ice or frozen rain), and at about 15 feet up with 20 feet still to go I came to a standstill. Then it all became clear and I felt the *adventura* that I had read about. I couldn't be timid anymore. Leaders don't always have a choice to step down and let someone else take the lead. After gathering my courage and realizing that I did trust my gear, I let my legs and arms find the balance I needed to climb the rest of the way. *(Grand Teton Mountaineering)*

- In climbing, the risks can be great and the consequences can be fatal. To function as part of a team, and to overcome those risks, you must trust and take responsibility for those in front of you as well as those behind you. On one pitch you are leading, and at the next, you are belaying. The continuous shifting of trust and responsibility strengthens a team. It is not too large a mental leap to transport the idea into business. Most businesses are structured hierarchically, and one has people above and below. A good leader will need not only to trust decisions from above, but also to take responsibility for those below. *(Grand Teton Mountaineering)*

In Practice

John Sims, partner, managing director and CFO at Snowden Lane Partners, a financial services firm, reflects on what mountain guides and his team members on a successful climb on the Grand Teton taught him about trust:

If you don't trust the person who has you on belay, chances are that you are not going to get very far. You may take much smaller incremental steps up the mountain face, only as far as you think you can get, trusting in your own ability. You will slowly inch your way up the mountain face. The rest of your team are all stuck behind you, unproductive, waiting for you to complete the climb as far as the rope will let you, until it is their turn to climb the same path, with the same trust only in their own abilities.

Without trust, you will be painstakingly slower. The team may run out of daylight well short of the intended goal. And so it will be in business. Without trust in your teammates, you will only do as much as your faith in your own limited abilities will take you. You will not risk stretching your own expertise or experience, and you are unlikely to learn as much from those around you. Each person will revert to being an island, placing trust only in his or her own abilities and therefore limiting individual and corporate horizons.

The Message

Guides help their charges build trust—in themselves, their equipment, and in their capacity to build trusting relationships with fellow climbers on their rope team. The many expedition members who wrote about trust in this chapter's sidebars truly experienced, in the most visceral of ways, what it meant to be linked together as they traversed new and unfamiliar territory. As one expedition participant memorably said, "If you cannot trust, you cannot climb." Read through the action steps to discover more ways to build trust.

ACTION STEPS FOR BUILDING TRUST

Trust, psychology professor Jeffry A. Simpson writes, may be the single most important ingredient for the development and maintenance of happy, well-functioning relationships. Trust involves an expectation that a partner's actions will be beneficial to one's long-term self-interest, and is higher when both partners' interests are well matched or when both believe the other will act on what's best for the relationship—even if their personal self-interests are different. Trust also increases as individuals move from having confidence in their partner's general predictability to having confidence in their values, motives, goals, and intentions. Simpson suggests four core principles of interpersonal trust:

- Individuals estimate trust by observing whether their partner makes decisions that might go against their own personal self-interest in order to support the relationship.
- Situations that test trusting relationships occur naturally in life—but may also be created by an individual to test whether a current level of trust is warranted.
- Individuals who are more securely attached, have higher self-esteem, and a clear sense of self should be more likely to experience trust as well as increases in trust in relationships across time.
- The dispositions and actions of both partners impact trust levels.[11]

Consider these action steps to help build trust:

- **Build relationships.**
  - Wharton legal studies professor G. Richard Shell and Mario Moussa, PhD, senior fellow at Wharton Executive Education, suggest these simple ways to build trust:

- *The similarity principle:* Studies have shown that we trust others a little more when we see them as familiar or similar to us—and these similarities don't have to go deep to smooth the way to better communication. Shell cites an experiment in which investigators set up a series of online negotiations between business students at two universities: half were given only their partner's name and told to begin the negotiation. The other half were given a photograph of their negotiation partner, and were instructed to use their initial communication to exchange social information. The result: 30 percent of the first group deadlocked at no deal, while just 6 percent of the group that exchanged social information ended in a deadlock.[12]
- *Gifts and favors:* Giving something as a symbol of good faith helps to establish trust. A gift, Shell says, is a symbol of an underlying relationship between two parties. Moreover, "gifts, kindnesses, and a thoughtful regard for other people's feelings are all ways of helping to establish and maintain close personal relationships—and the same acts carry symbolic weight at the bargaining table even though the relationships there may be more professional than personal in character."[13]
- *Relationships:* Shell and Moussa write that "relationships give people a level of trust and confidence in each other, facilitating communication and making it easier to cooperate." Establishing or reestablishing rapport and taking an interest in others can help build a foundation of trust. "People respond well to—and remember—others who take an interest in them, especially when there is no obvious strategic benefit that flows from that interaction." Shell also says the mere fact that we share a mutual acquaintance with our counterpart may help us appear more familiar and establish a minimal condition for trust. The bottom line: Develop the habit of using similarity and liking to build goodwill.[14]
- **Build a high-performance team based on trust.**
  - Tom Pandola and James Bird together accumulated almost 50 years of firefighting experience in the Los Angeles City Firefighting Department. What they learned about leadership, teamwork, and trust in such critical environments applies well to any team faced with complexity and challenge:
    - High-performance teamwork demands components like trusted inspirational leadership and a culture that rewards people for expanding their comfort zone for risk-taking. "People will only take risks," they say, "if there is trust and confidence between team members and, more importantly, between the rank-and-file members and their leaders."
    - A culture of consistent and common purpose is key. Trusted leaders must be perceived as consistent, so their teams can anticipate how leaders will react to challenges. From consistency comes confidence.
    - Knowing what is expected from each team member can lead to an inner strength that comes from a shared purpose. "These dynamics have the

power to morph into teamwork," the authors say. "Trusted teamwork eventually sows mutual respect. No team member, or anyone else for that matter, wants to fail or disappoint anyone with whom he or she shares mutual respect; mutual respect is the cornerstone for any high-performance team."[15]

- **Show your human side.**
  - Harvard Business School professor Amy J.C. Cuddy and her co-authors Matthew Kohut and John Neffinger say that to exert influence, you must balance competence with warmth. Most leaders, they write, tend to emphasize their strength, competence, and credentials. But leaders who project strength before establishing trust run the risk of eliciting fear. To lead effectively, the authors suggest beginning with warmth, which they term the "conduit of influence." Warmth facilitates "trust and the communication and absorption of ideas . . . Prioritizing warmth helps you connect immediately with those around you, demonstrating that you hear them, understand them, and can be trusted by them." To project warmth, Cuddy and her co-authors suggest aiming for a tone that suggests you're leveling with people, share a personal story, validate others' feelings, and aim for a natural, unforced, smile.[16]

- **Communicate your character.**
  - Wharton management professor Mike Useem says that the key to effectively establishing trust is the ability to communicate your character. With trust, he says, "you've got more latitude as a leader, you can get more things done. You can act quickly without having to explain everything yet again. If people have confidence in who you are, they trust you." But trustworthiness has to be demonstrated through action—just *telling* people to trust you won't get the job done. "It's a matter of consistently communicating your good character," he says, "as well as the character of everybody all the way down to the front line."[17]

- **Cues to trustworthiness.**
  - Northeastern University psychologist David DeSteno suggests that a useful way to think about trust is to consider whether you are focused on gaining benefits in the *moment* or benefits in the *future*. A decision to be untrustworthy could certainly lead to quick gains—but more than likely won't maximize long-term outcomes. From this perspective the ability to *self-regulate*, "to resist immediate desires in favor of those that possess long-term benefit," becomes an important aspect of trustworthiness.[18]
  - DeSteno's laboratory experiments involving pairs of strangers asked to play an economic game revealed that certain cues, *when taken together*, were strongly predictive of trustworthiness. The more frequently a partner engaged in crossing arms, leaning away, face touching, and hand touching, the less trustworthy he or she acted during the experiment.[19,20]
  - Are there observable signals of competency, and do they send signals of trustworthiness to others? Members of groups participating in laboratory

experiments reported wanting to follow individuals who signaled pride and confidence through their posture and upward head tilt. "In terms of competence," DeSteno reports, "this suggests that as long as a person truly believes she is qualified, she'll emit cues that signal she can be trusted." He adds, of course, that if her assessment is misguided, so too will be others' perceptions, for signaling "is all about intention and belief: it's not always tied to objective facts."[21]

NINE

Guides Manage Risk in an Environment of Uncertainty

Finding the balance between risk and safety

Climb if you will, but remember that courage and strength are nought without prudence, and that a momentary negligence may destroy the happiness of a lifetime. Do nothing in haste; look well to each step; and from the beginning think what may be the end.

—EDWARD WHYMPER

PARTICIPANT: Can I go closer to the edge?
MOUNTAIN GUIDE: Yes, of course. Thanks for asking, though.

Guides know that risk is an inherent part of mountain sports, yet also know that clients actually want to experience the very real mental and physical challenges that these activities offer. Describing the visceral sensation of climbing, an article that guide Al Read and I wrote some years ago for the *Wharton Leadership Digest* began:

> Tie onto the end of the rope, step off the ledge, and you are committed to the climb. All of your senses suddenly come into focus. The wind is louder in your ears, the rock rougher beneath your fingers, the smell of your own sweat sharper in your nostrils. Adrenaline flows, and you tingle with the thrill of meeting nature's wildest challenges. You have voluntarily entered the realm of high adventure.[1]

While guiding Yang Sun and her climbing party on the Grand Teton, Exum guide Christian Santelices worked closely with guide Amy Carse to balance Sun's firm determination to continue the climb against the ever-present issues of risk and uncertainty. In Exum's practice with novice climbers, the guide goes first, and a team of three or four climbers follows. Carse says, "My job is to keep my clients safe, that's the number one thing. If I have a client who is not fit enough, or if there are afternoon thunderstorms, or they are not ready to take on the responsibilities it involves, then I can just say, '*It's not safe for you, it's not your time*,' and they respect that."

Exum's Jack Tackle agrees:

> In my function as a guide, my number-one job is safety. Every decision I make is based on that. It's about managing acceptable risk, and making good decisions, but also being fluid in the process, to keep making sure that you're making good decisions, not being afraid to turn around and go down. You can't be set in a preordained style and keep pushing because summit fever has kicked in.

Guides also recognize that clients have invested time, energy, and resources in preparing for their adventure. On the Grand Teton climb with Yang Sun, guides Santelices and Carse worked hard to balance issues of risk and uncertainty with their client's desire to continue her climb. Their decision to help Yang reach the West Summit was a win–win for all parties.

Participant Reflections

- When standing at the foot of a mountain, one is essentially faced with two choices; accept the challenge and go for the summit, or turn around, go home and admire the mountain from a distance. For many, climbing a mountain does not appear to present them with any useful or practical lessons, only the thrill of the experience and much "unnecessary" exposure to risk. This argument seems logical. Why put yourself in a position with seemingly little to gain and yet everything to lose? The fact is though, that the mountains have an incredible amount to offer us and there are a multitude of lessons that can be learned from climbing and facing adversity on a mountain. Pushing your physical limits; learning new levels of trust in ourselves, our teammates and our equipment; learning to make decisive yet informed decisions; working cohesively in a team of strangers; learning when to step in and out of leadership roles; strengthening one's interpersonal relations and ability to get on with others; these are just a handful of critical lessons that one can learn. However, I would like to highlight one particular lesson that stood out for me. That was the notion of taking *small steps* towards reaching your goal. It is a simple and often overlooked skill that is applicable both on a mountain and in business and our everyday environment. In climbing, the idea of taking baby steps comes about from the fact that by moving just a few inches upwards, you can now see the rock face from a new perspective and see holds that were not as clear to you before. It is also important to *keep* moving. In light of the speed at which conditions change in the mountains, even a small movement is a positive movement. On top of this, taking smaller steps acts to reduce risk even in situations where one's overall exposure to risk is extremely high. When traversing, and there is drop of several hundred feet below, taking small movements is far safer than trying to take a giant leap. In business, the same logic applies. There is less risk in tackling the smaller goal in front of you than trying to jump to larger conclusions that you may not have the appropriate information to make. In both cases, by taking the smaller step you are making a positive movement towards your goal, while at the same time reducing the risk of making a mistake, which in many cases could have hazardous consequences both for you and your team. *(Grand Teton Mountaineering)*

- Perhaps the most important lesson learned before the trip even began dealt with the risks involved. As a nursing student, we have been taught to assess risk in almost every task we undertake. For instance, before lifting or transferring a patient, I must assess the potential risks involving both of us before proceeding. Since I have read a few mountaineering books and have a handful of climbing friends, I knew of the lengthy list of risks involved in undertaking a climb up the Grand Teton. Given the reality that I tend to be somewhat of a "safety-first" individual and that I had never experienced a technical climb before, my perceived risk of this venture was probably greater than that of a daredevil who has successfully summited K2. However, I felt the risks were an essential aspect of the adventure, and I wanted to be removed from my comfort zone in order to fully challenge myself both physically (where there was the risk of serious injury) and mentally (where there was the risk of self-doubt and failure). *(Grand Teton Mountaineering)*

Uncertainty is an elusive term that has numerous conceptualizations. Raanan Lipshitz and Orna Strauss of the University of Haifa discuss the impact of uncertainty on decision making. Uncertainty in the context of action, they write, is a sense of doubt that blocks or delays action. Decision makers are confronted with doubts about alternatives, outcomes, and even the nature of the situation, due to incomplete or conflicting information, or equally attractive (or unattractive) alternatives. Strategies for coping with uncertainty include reducing, acknowledging, or suppressing it.[2] Guides apply elements of at least the first two of these strategies, bringing knowledge gained over many years in the field to bear on the decision at hand, reducing variability by insisting on procedures such as standardized communication protocols between climbers, by using familiar routes, and by careful advance preparation.

We learned in earlier chapters that conditions of uncertainty hold growth opportunities, too. Experienced guides leverage uncertainty to provide expedition participants with rich opportunities for meaningful decision making and teamwork, such as route finding, thereby enhancing the leadership development components of an already challenging trek in unfamiliar territory. Risk and uncertainty play a key part in many business decisions, too. Paul Asel, a professional in the venture capital and private equity field, notes that a tolerance for risk is essential for entrepreneurs. He writes, "Entrepreneurs have learned to embrace risk as the catalyst for new business opportunity for one simple reason: Uncertainty is the handmaiden of opportunity. Disruptive economic or technological change is a greenhouse for new companies, as entrepreneurial initiative, innovation, and nimbleness can overcome the traditional advantages of established firms during these uncertain periods."[3]

Exum guide Doug Coombs, talking about guiding on steep snow slopes, said:

> My theory is that a good guide keeps a person at his level and a little over it. If you keep a client at his level, or a little under, he is going to go home saying, *"That was a great experience, it's very safe. I didn't learn a lot, but I had a good time and I was safe."* But if I push him a little harder than he would himself, you know, get him out of his little envelope, his bubble, well, you can watch the awareness grow. People become more aware of everything because they learned.

Exum guide Mark Newcomb adds:

> We offer opportunity to experience risk—that's a big part of it. When people come to climb a mountain, what they are getting themselves into is a situation in which they feel uncomfortable and they may perceive a large risk. You can look way down below and imagine yourself sort of pitching over the edge. When clients start to feel overly worried about the exposure, to the point where they are not doing the right thing, perhaps freezing up a bit, letting their fear get the best of them, leaning in to the rock too much, I try to break it down into really small steps for them. *"Take one step back; find a place where you can completely relax."* The goal is to find a way to move to the next piece of ground where you are comfortable. I might say, *"That space is an irregular edge, but it's larger than the curb you stand on every day for the bus!"*

Vertical's Gabriel Becker says:

Clients need to know and understand the risks. What I tell them is that we try to do our best in security, we have the right training, and we have the tools to help you confront whatever we face. But we also really try to enjoy what we are doing, and we tell clients, "*You don't need to stress so much.*" We allow them to experience what is happening all around them, to go just beyond the boundaries of comfort, but only to that area and then bounce back, come back to comfort. We try to be in the "aware area" all the time.

Exum's Al Read agrees:

You're trying to give clients a safe experience, but climbing is not safe. You ride a razor's edge of safety versus daring, and you try not to turn into the dangerous side, or if you do, you try to get back to the other side of it. The very nature of climbing is doing something that could be very dangerous. If you didn't have that, it wouldn't be climbing. It wouldn't be the same thing. As you are going up you are assessing this, because it's something clients will remember all of their lives.

Participant Reflections

- We started our first day by learning basic knots and belaying techniques. After lunch, they took us to the mountainside in groups to apply the lessons. My team quickly ascended two easy pitches while demonstrating both enthusiasm for the climb and care for the rules of safety. After reaching the top of the cliff face, our guide prepared us for rappel practice—one of the most exciting and dangerous parts of the climbing experience. After I took my turn walking backward down the vertical rock, I returned to the ledge and relaxed, admiring the view. Careless, looking at the horizon rather than my feet, I stumbled while stepping past a rappel rope. After the second time this occurred, our team's guide pulled me aside. "The difference between climbing and other exercise," the guide stated, "is how consequential the actions of an individual can be for an entire team. A single stumble over a rope can lead to a fall concluding in severe injury or death. Showing care on the mountainside is critical, but that same level of attention is required until each member of the team is completely off the mountain." The guide took a minute to ensure I understood the point and would keep it in mind; he spoke to me seriously and respectfully, watching me acknowledge his words. (*Grand Teton Mountaineering*)

- I have come to realize how physical challenges can truly bring people of different backgrounds and personalities together. When faced with the inherent risks and difficulties of outdoor adventure, people must lay down their guard in an effort to find trust and companionship in those surrounding them. They will hope to find comfort in their fellow adventure seekers because they are the only ones who will face the same mental and physical tests. In this process, each begins playing their own role, taking up their own tasks, and making their abilities to trust, respect, and lead apparent. *(Grand Teton Mountaineering)*

• Keep a close lookout for those needing additional help. If some are not in danger and are coping well enough, you can let them do their thing. When it gets serious, or the weather looks threatening, you can step in to prevent injury or pick up the pace to avoid unnecessary risk. Risk management is about assessing the potential problems, making a conscious decision what to live with and what actions to take to minimize unacceptable risks, and then performing within those parameters. The guide decides what to allow the clients to do, how far to leave them to their own devices and when to step in, either teaching or dictating, as the circumstances demand. A manager can do something similar, empowering an employee with accountability and responsibility, without destroying the individual's ability or desire to take initiative. *(Grand Teton Mountaineering)*

Why do some of us choose to undertake the very real risks involved in outdoor sports? In 1990, sociologist Stephen Lyng described *edgework*, a concept encompassing voluntary risk-taking in activities as diverse and challenging as skiing, automobile racing, skydiving, mountaineering, and business entrepreneurship—even wartime combat:

> While there seems to be general agreement among members of contemporary American society about the value of reducing threats to individual well-being, there are many who actively seek experiences that involve a high potential for personal injury or death . . . (edgework) allows us to view high-risk behavior as involving, most fundamentally, the problem of negotiating the boundary between chaos and order.[4]

While one psychological model of risk-taking views anticipated rewards as the primary motivation for risk-taking behavior, Lyng notes that in voluntary risk taking some place a higher value on the *experience* of risk taking than they do on a successful outcome. Those choosing to work on the "edge" seek to define the limits of performance, whether in technology, body, or mind. But their choice to engage in risk-taking activities is a calculated one:

> Edgeworkers are not typically interested in thrill-seeking or gambling because they dislike placing themselves in threatening situations involving circumstances they cannot control. . . . What they seek is the chance to exercise skills in negotiating a challenge rather than turn their fate over to the roll of the dice. . . . The first challenge is to negotiate one's way past hazards that can be anticipated. But the ultimate challenge is to survive those hazards that cannot be anticipated, that require the use of one's innate survival capacity.[5]

Philip Ebert and Simon Robertson, both philosophy professors and avid mountaineers in the United Kingdom, say that while many non-climbers carry a stereotyped image of mountaineers as risk-seeking climbers, mountaineers acknowledge that there are risks but tend to regard these risks as "acceptable." Reasons for these differences, they suggest, include a "desensitization" of mountaineers to reports of climbing-related injuries, media bias that dramatizes mountaineering disasters while less frequently covering mountaineering successes, and the possibility that non-mountaineers, who have no positive emotional attachment to the activity, may recall only emotionally distressing outcomes, and thus judge the risks higher than do mountaineers.[6]

Competence also comes into the picture: mountaineers become more "in tune" with the risks involved, Ebert and Robertson say, by developing the skills to identify, assess, and manage them. It all comes down to this—are the kinds of risks that mountaineers willingly take on justified? Their answer is that "engaging with mountaineering risks has value . . . when the risk is taken and overcome competently."[7] The benefits, they propose, include a heightened focus upon and appreciation of both oneself and one's surroundings and a sense of exhilaration, which leads to a sense of personal fulfillment, as well as a sense of experiencing oneself as an effective agent in the chosen environment. This latter statement supports guide Doug Coombs's thoughts about his clients' growth of awareness during challenging guided experiences.

Mountaineer and guide Gaston Rébuffat lamented, "In this modern age, very little remains that is real. Night has been banished, so have the cold, the wind and the stars."[8] Much of our exposure to risk, says Anthony Giddens, has been disembedded—lifted out of our modern experience—and replaced with expert systems in which we place faith.[9] Exum guide Jack Turner agrees that in our daily lives we are often protected or insulated from risk by a variety of experts, such as financial advisors, real estate agents, and career counselors. However, when venturing up a mountain, uncertainties become much more directly experienced.[10] Turner says:

> An awful lot of American life is designed so you can live your life without *anything* at stake. Even if something is at stake, it's money or numbers flying by on a computer. Climbing involves you in a very direct way, where you have responsibility for someone else. There's something tremendously real with climbing, confronting something where you have to pay attention, where you want your companions to pay attention. That is particularly so for those who do everything they can to avoid taking a risk. Climbing is like walking into a mirrored room in which you take all that and project it onto the mirror and you find that things are very real, and if you screw up somebody can get killed or badly hurt.

Guides assess risks and uncertainty posed by the weather, the route, conditions on the mountain, and the skills of the client in a way that provides as much safety as is humanly possible while operating in an environment of constant threat and change. While seasoned mountaineers may not require a guide, for less experienced climbers a guide with a finely honed sense of survival, long experience, and leadership skills in full play is the mediator between risk and survival. Guides work hard to find the right balance between allowing the client to experience an acceptable level of risk and uncertainty and knowing when the time is right to turn around.

Participant Reflections

- In the mountains you have to learn to trust your own two feet, your personal judgment, and, perhaps most importantly, to trust your climbing partner. I asked guide Jack Turner to define leadership. His answer: "Leadership is a capacity for risk and trust." *(Grand Teton Mountaineering)*

- Risk was what I thought the whole trip was about. Leaders take risk and are rewarded—although the reward could be a lesson learned. *(Grand Teton Mountaineering)*

- On this venture I was confronted with challenges in which I had to take risks. Whether it was meeting and trusting a new group, learning the new skill of rock climbing, or trusting new people and equipment, these risks all showed me that placing myself in my "yellow zone," or on the verge of uncomfortable, is necessary to become a better leader. The important caveat to taking risks is having enough trust and confidence in yourself *and* in your community. I chose this quote by Don Mellor because I believe it captures my greatest leadership lesson from the trip:
  Climbing is a metaphor for life itself. There is the aspiration and the uncertainty, the journey and the risk, the success and its concomitant satisfaction. Life on the wall becomes a simplified model of life in the harried world, a model with equal anguish, but one whose challenges are carved into perfect definition. We win here and we know we can win elsewhere. *(Grand Teton Mountaineering)*

- The ability or degree to which we take risk becomes entirely dependent on trust. In the dialogue between climber and belayer, one person is consciously saying, "I trust you with my life." The other person responds with "I accept your trust and I will not drop you." *(Grand Teton Mountaineering)*

In Practice

Lyndsey Bunting, now a senior financial analyst at Birchbox after a stint in investment banking in New York City and service as a Peace Corps volunteer in the mountains of Panama, made two summit attempts on the Grand Teton. She fell ill at 11,650 feet on her first try, but successfully motivated and led her team of climbers to the summit on her second ascent a year later. Bunting says:

There is a paradox with climbing and mountaineering, in general. You seek out these experiences that push you to your physical edge and represent some sort of danger to your person—whether that's climbing a challenging route on the Grand Teton or Mount Everest. That's where the thrill lives, when something significant is at risk. At the same time, you and your guide are actively doing everything that you can to mitigate those risks.

It's this idea of jumping in—fully aware of the risks that you face and jumping in nonetheless—and making decisions that minimize those risks and address those threats. The element of risk-taking applies to startups in particular. In working at a startup there is risk and uncertainty, and correctly weighing those against the potential benefits can make all the difference. The team that you build is important, and you have to trust those individuals to also make good decisions on your behalf. One of our guides on the Grand Teton said that you can't hide on the mountain, meaning that every fall was public. He mentioned that for relationships where there was a clear hierarchy (for example, boss to employee) this experience was often most difficult for the person in a position of power. No one wants to fail, and it's even harder when there is an imbalance of power in the relationship. On a more positive note, he said that you could always tell a strong relationship when neither partner is afraid to fail—when someone isn't embarrassed to fall, dusts off, and gets back up again with the support of their partner.

I think that individuals can learn to deal with ambiguity and uncertainty. Whether it's a skill that we've had to learn from a tough life, like many of the world's poorest populations, or something that we seek to learn through mountain climbing or other pursuits, functioning and thriving in uncertainty is something that we're all able to learn. I think that is the value of climbing mountains or living in a developing country—we learn to deal with uncertainty. I firmly believe that the more that you challenge yourself in uncertain conditions, understand your resistance and, more importantly, your reaction to elements outside of your control, the better equipped you are to deal with them in all aspects of your life.

The Message

To me, mountaineer Gaston Rébuffat's lament that "in this modern age very little remains that is real" is, at its heart, a call to seek out the high peaks and tough challenges that still await beyond the comforts of modern life. And this is why Lyndsey Bunting's uplifting thoughts about engaging with uncertainty and risk at work and in life continue to inspire me. It would have been more straightforward, and certainly less personally risky, for her to remain at her job in investment banking in New York City—but she chose to take a different path, served in the Peace Corps, and returned to New York with a deeper appreciation of how to thrive in an uncertain world.

Guides work hard to help their clients overcome their fears of falling (or failing) by understanding the terrain, knowing the route, appreciating weather patterns, and balancing the doubt that creeps into decision making in conditions of uncertainty with measured experience and thoughtful action. Read through the action steps that follow for some advice on managing risk and uncertainty in your own environment.

ACTION STEPS FOR MANAGING RISK

The term "risk," Anthony Giddens says, is a relatively modern construction, and derives from an understanding that unanticipated results may be a consequence of our own actions, rather than mere fortune. The word "risk," according to Giddens, found its way into English in the 17th century, and likely comes from a Spanish nautical term meaning to run into danger or to go against a rock.[11] Psychologist Daniel Kahneman points out that in life most options we face include a risk of loss and an opportunity for gain. How our options are framed matters: "When directly compared or weighted against each other," Kahneman says, "losses loom larger than gains. This asymmetry between the power of positive and negative expectations or experiences has an evolutionary history. Organisms that treat threats as more urgent than opportunities have a better chance to survive and reproduce."[12]

We're not without some really good tools to manage risk. Advance planning, expertise, and good judgment are key, and new research offers ways to dramatically reduce risk. Some experts write about risk from a very broad perspective; others take a more local view. Ian Bremmer, president of a political-risk consulting group, takes a broad and worldly perspective on risk, saying that while business leaders routinely analyze the economic risk of overseas ventures, in today's complex environment they now also need to look closely at *political* risk, which is more subjective than its economic counterpart.[13] Wharton professors Howard Kunreuther and Mike Useem look carefully at the risk assessment, risk perception, and risk management aspects of low-probability, high-consequence events such as Hurricane Katrina, reminding us that, in their words, "low risk is not no risk."[14]

One key recommendation from Kunreuther and Useem fits our topic particularly well: Build leadership for averting and responding to disasters before it is needed. I can attest to the importance of this latter point. In 1979, I worked in a general hospital located just 10 miles from the Three Mile Island (TMI) nuclear power plant. At 4 a.m. on March 28, the nuclear reactor in TMI Unit 2 experienced a partial meltdown, quickly becoming the most serious accident in U.S. commercial nuclear power plant operating history. For several days following the accident, the population living in the area was subjected to conflicting reports from both plant and government officials, and, most alarming of all, to the news of a hydrogen bubble trapped in the dome of the pressure vessel—the container that held the damaged reactor core itself. During the incident, planning for emergency evacuation was rapidly expanded from the existing 5-mile risk zone, which contained no medical facilities and just 3 nursing homes, to a 20-mile zone around the plant, which included 14 hospitals and 62 nursing homes. An article I later published in the *American Journal of Public Health* reported how area hospitals responded by rapidly discharging noncritical patients and crash planning for the possible evacuation and transport of more seriously ill patients. I described this kind of accident as "nontraditional" (consider that emergency response systems usually focus on getting patients *into* the hospital, rather than the reverse), and without "clearly defined limits of time and space."[15] Toxic waste accidents, terrorist events, and other phenomena without historical precedent also fit this description. Although the accident was successfully contained within several days and the reactor eventually permanently shut down, the event at TMI brought into focus for many that we live side by side with risk and uncertainty, and that we must deal with it.

These, of course, are the big and scary events we see on the news, which often result in large-scale response, and are then quickly replaced by news of the next emerging concern. But closer to home and our own experience, the humble checklist (discussed below) has had an enormous impact in reducing risk in airliners, surgical suites, in the construction industry—even in investment management.[16] And, finally, as leadership experts all too often remind us, building a disciplined team that works well together before an emergency strikes is very wise advice.

Consider these action steps to manage risk:

- **Use a checklist.**
  - Atul Gawande, MD, a Harvard Medical School professor and surgeon, says in his book *The Checklist Manifesto* that avoidable failures are common and persistent across many fields because "the volume and complexity of what we know has exceeded our individual ability to deliver its benefits correctly, safely, and reliably." Medicine, he says, has "become the art of managing extreme complexity" in an era of superspecialists. His recommendation is remarkably simple—use a checklist. Developed by military pilots in the 1930s after the preventable crash of a long-range bomber during a test flight, a simple checklist that includes the minimum necessary steps for a given process helps with memory recall and dramatically reduces failures. One interesting approach, taken by what Gawande describes as an ordinary community hospital attempting to improve its emergency response to drownings, was to give checklists to the people with the least power in the whole process— the pre-hospital rescue squads and the telephone operator—who then were better able to provide the advance notification so desperately needed by the hospital's surgical team. While checklists generally dictate instructions downward, they can also, Gawande says, push the power of decision making in complex, nonroutine problems out to the periphery and away from the center, allowing for creativity and adaptation while still ensuring careful documentation. One set of checklists ensures that critical items aren't missed: a second set ensures communication and accountability between the players. Other checklists, for airline pilots or surgical teams, for example, are tightly focused on the critical steps of the principals. What does a good checklist look like? Gawande advises to keep the checklist practical, precise, efficient, to the point, and easy to use in challenging situations, providing reminders of only the most critical and important steps.[17]
  - Marine Lt. Col. Phil Treglia, a former member of the Marines' Force Recon, developed a set of rules designed to protect him and his team on the ground in Iraq and Afghanistan. One of his rules was to work through a checklist written on a three-by-five card before embarking on patrol: check the driver,

check unsecured items in the vehicle, check under seats for anything loose that might become a projectile if the vehicle was hit, and more. Treglia knew from hard experience that trouble on an operation was always a possibility—and he used his checklist to effectively minimize what risks he could.[18]

• Wharton management professor Mike Useem developed a checklist to help business leaders under pressure make effective decisions. Among the mission-critical principles that Useem recommends: express confidence in and support for those you lead, communicate persuasively, emphasize the group's common purpose, and act decisively.[19]

- **Extend your comfort zone.**
  - The National Outdoor Leadership School (NOLS) teaches "tolerance for adversity and uncertainty" through its rigorous outdoor experiences. John Kanengieter, a consultant, educator, and director of leadership for NOLS, and Aparna Rajagopal-Durbin, a NOLS faculty member, write in the *Harvard Business Review* that despite careful planning for expeditions, many factors simply can't be known in advance. Weather can change rapidly in the mountains, the condition of the trail ahead is unknown, and both the mental and physical endurance of the team are sure to be tested along the way. NOLS tells participants to "plan for things they can control, let go of things they can't, expect the unexpected, and maintain composure when it arrives." Building tolerance for adversity and uncertainty applies in the workplace, too, as entrepreneurs and managers need to be prepared to meet unexpected challenges with steadiness. Kanengieter and Rajagopal-Durban say learning from the lessons of outdoor exploration can teach one to look past the immediate danger and distraction and focus attention on the most important tasks at hand without panicking.[20]

- **Share the risk you ask others to take.**
  - Brigadier General Thomas Kolditz (U.S. Army, retired), a former professor at the U.S. Military Academy and now a leadership professor at the Yale School of Management, knows a lot about leading while in imminent physical danger. In addition to his military assignments worldwide, he headed up the department of behavioral science and leadership at West Point, and served as mentor and coach to the U.S. Military Academy sport parachute team. Leadership in such situations, Kolditz writes, involves a "profound and consistent sharing of risk." Contrasting this level of shared risk with the protections commonly afforded top business executives, Kolditz says, "Shared risk makes the organization more survivable and the leader more trusted by his followers."[21]

- **Don't gamble it all away!**
  - It is no surprise that mountaineers and guides deal with risk every time they set out. Gaston Rébuffat, the French mountaineer, guide, and member of Maurice Herzog's triumphant 1950 Annapurna expedition, tells us "that men in this age of easy living should be attracted by difficulty is a logical and

just reaction. In contrast to the ordered world of towns, mountains offer the realm of the unknown. That is a delight that not even the oldest climbers can exhaust. But danger, that is quite another matter! The real mountaineer does not like taking risks. It is stupid to scorn death. We are too fond of life to gamble it away. In my profession of guide, I have to accept some risks every day. I know them too well, I fear them too much to like them or seek them out. No, make sure you do the hardest and most daring things as safely as possible!"[22]

- These key risk management tips from a leading source for mountaineers also apply well to the decisions leaders must make at ground level:
  - Keep alert to clues that you may be losing full awareness of your situation, including failure to meet planned targets like start time or turnaround time. In mountaineering, pushing for the summit beyond a preset turnaround time can lead to disaster. In business, continuing to invest in a failing project can have the same result.
  - Check your stress levels: a moderate level of stress can help you make good decisions, while a very low level of stress can breed complacency and inattention.
  - Most climbing accidents result from a combination of circumstances, rather than from a single cause. Mountaineers call it the "poor-judgment chain." One poor judgment call increases the probability that another will follow.
  - Seek feedback on your decisions. Open communication in the team makes all the difference.[23]

TEN

Guides See the Big Picture

The meaning of the journey

If you get to the summit, it's great. If not, it's great also.
—VERTICAL GUIDE WILLIE PARRA

A good leader needs to not only learn to motivate a group to persevere, but also to know when to help a group to take a step back and move in a different direction.
—EXPEDITION PARTICIPANT

On Cerro Escudo, climber Chris Breemer got it right when he finally reached the top of the sheer wall, looked to his left along a ridge of rotten rock, spied the summit, and called it a day. Breemer acknowledged, "We were done. The wall was climbed and we had no desire to slap the summit."[1]

Guides develop an acute perspective on the importance of the journey on the way to and from the summit, and for them a great journey *is* the prize. Guides work hard to pass this perspective on to their charges, too. On the Grand Teton climb with Yang Sun, Christian Santelices clearly understood Sun's journey, and proposed an alternative that helped her to reach her own summit while deftly balancing guide Amy Carse's concern for safety for her team. For Santelices and his team on Cerro Escudo, and for many other mountaineers who have had to make a similar decision when the summit is within reach, the right call can mean the difference between life and death.

British mountaineer Stephen Venables writes about reaching the summit of Mount Everest:

> Ideally you arrive in the early morning to enjoy luminous clarity. Late in the afternoon, I had to content myself with immense depths glimpsed through swirling clouds and the first falling snowflakes. But who cares? The views are always better on the way up. And in any case, the summit is not the glorious climax; it is simply the point when you are furthest from base, like the astronauts in their lunar module, wanting only to return to Earth. . . . Then, facing into the wind, I forced my flagging body to carry on down, knowing that the real struggle had only just begun.[2]

Participant Reflections

- "It's not about the summit, it's about the journey." How many times have you heard these words repeated? Why is the journey arguably the most important component of any task? Think about it from the reverse. Let us say that you are solely focused on the summit, and are exerting all your energy into achieving this one goal. Fair enough, but what happens if, for whatever reason, this objective is not achieved? By singling out this goal as the sole purpose of your task, you are setting yourself up for severe disappointment and let-down if it is not achieved, and will consider it nothing more than an utter waste of time. However, by focusing on the journey, you are learning and further developing yourself as both a team player and as an individual as the task unfolds. There are so many opportunities for development as you move from one stage to the next, but if you do not consider these as goals unto themselves rather than as a means to an end, they will be forgotten by the wayside. Furthermore, concentrating on the journey enhances your enjoyment through the entire process. While hiking up the mountain to our campground for the night, we took the opportunity to gaze at the amazing vistas, look for wildlife, and joke with one another. Perhaps this meant we were not moving as quickly as we could have been, but it did not matter in the slightest, and we now have a collection of great stories that we will keep with us in the future. *(Grand Teton Mountaineering)*

- Our trek provided a unique understanding of leadership and teamwork because, enveloped in a breathtakingly beautiful natural environment and largely isolated from contact with those at home, I was able to keep our venture's physical and intellectual goals at the forefront of my mind. Perhaps, for all of us, the relative isolation and unfamiliar terrain ultimately fostered a greater sense of collaborative purpose than I ever experienced as a member of the many athletic teams I have been a part of throughout my life. We were working towards one common, exciting and very real goal—summiting the glacier. Accordingly, our team certainly transformed over the course of the experience: what started out as a group of near-strangers grew to become teammates literally bound to one another by ropes and harnesses, working together to reach the summit. *(Iceland)*

- As we begin our descent down the mountain, I become aware of silences that hadn't existed yesterday—everyone is struggling with the same feelings as me but understands the harm of voicing them publicly. One of our team, exhausted, is progressing slowly as we descend into a steep talus field. I tentatively try to remark on the beauty of the fog. As I describe it, a strange sensation fills me. Inspired, I continue to look around for things to appreciate. The new rivulets made by the constant downpour. The mist climbing up the glacier. The sound of rocks falling in a distant chute. As I enumerate the beauty in the scenery, I start to feel peacefully happy. And I notice the most remarkable effect on our weary team member— the more I talk, the more quickly and confidently she descends the mountain. In effect, we distract ourselves into a successful descent, so that I summit something entirely different than the top of the mountain. *(Grand Teton Mountaineering)*

Summit fever, and the risks of descending in unsafe conditions, can lead to disaster. At 29,035 feet above sea level, the summit of Mount Everest is the highest point on earth. A recent study published in the *British Medical Journal* of mortality on Mount Everest over an 86-year period revealed that of the 94 mountaineers who died after climbing above 26,000 feet, 9 were climbing towards the summit and 16 had turned back short of the summit. The largest number who died, 53, were *descending* from the summit.[3]

Michael A. Roberto, a management professor at Bryant University, explains in the *California Management Review* that the tragedy that occurred on Mount Everest on May 10, 1996, in which two experienced expedition leaders, Rob Hall and Scott Fischer, and three of their clients died during a nighttime descent from the summit in a howling storm (made famous by Jon Krakauer's book *Into Thin Air*[4]), provides learning opportunities that extend well beyond the realm of mountain climbing. Roberto suggests that the interaction of cognitive biases, group dynamics, and system complexity contributed to the disaster.[5]

Cognitive biases, such as overconfidence, which impaired the judgment of the Everest expedition leaders; a tendency to focus on recent events such as the generally favorable weather on the mountain in the past several climbing seasons; and a failure to ignore sunk costs (in this context, pressure to make an ill-advised push for the summit due to the substantial investment already made in the effort) had a good deal to do with the loss of life during the descent. Sunk costs, in particular, are identified by Roberto as a major factor: The expedition leaders had repeatedly emphasized the need to turn around from a summit attempt at a pre-established time, but both failed to adhere to their own rule, allowing many climbers to reach the summit well behind schedule. The unfortunate result was a forced nighttime descent in a deadly storm.[6]

Roberto also identified a lack of psychological safety and poor team learning behavior as contributing factors to the Everest disaster, and he pointedly argues that team members (and some guides, too) did not feel comfortable expressing dissenting views. Without open discussion and encouragement to voice opinions within the team, most of the expedition climbers continued up to the summit despite their earlier agreement to a fixed turnaround time. Expedition members had little time to build trust in each other, and Roberto suggests that they never really coalesced as a team. Roberto also notes that very little slack existed in the system, as all expeditions gathered at base camp had agreed to a very tight 18-hour schedule for team summit attempts. Finally, the interaction of complex systems such as human errors, team procedures, equipment failures, and the wild storm all contributed to the tragedy in some way.[7] Roberto's message for organizational leaders is clear: build and develop teams before a crisis develops, encourage team members to speak up, don't let sunk costs dictate a perilous path to the summit—and keep a clear eye on the big picture.

Participant Reflections

- This climb has definitely been a series of ups and downs for everyone. Unlike previous expeditions, every member of the team managed to reach the Lower Saddle, and all were prepared for the final assault on the summit. The only thing that prevented us from reaching the summit was the weather. Disappointment was deep in our hearts as we watched the lightning streak across the dark and ominous skies. The guides looked grim but did not say anything, and we all held our silence, trusting their knowledge of the mountains. Eventually, the guides said that we had to head down. I'm sure all of us were disappointed, but we all hid it in our hearts and greeted each other with smiles, reveling in the fact that we had made it up so far. Many members of the group cheered us with their wisecracks and jokes, and none revealed any dejection. As for myself, I learned to appreciate the magnificent view around me. The stormy weather had veiled the mountains in mist, presenting a dreamy landscape that was simply astounding. This was a view that I had not seen on the first sunny day and would not have seen if I had been glum as I made the descent. Optimism definitely made all the difference. We will all face disappointments in our lives but it is how we approach it that makes all the difference. Some might wallow in depression, while others will stand up and look forward to the next challenge. (Grand Teton Mountaineering)

- While the importance of perseverance is an important lesson in leadership, I want to focus on something that's a little more subtle and less obvious and, because of its more elusive nature, is all the more important. We did not make it to the top.

And, as our guide said, we learned just as much as if we had. He said when he first was learning how to guide, he hoped for bad weather because he wanted to have a challenge—he wanted to be tested and persevere. As he became more experienced, he learned that knowing when to quit and turn back was even more important than knowing how to keep a group going and motivated. Persevering to get to a goal is one thing, but sometimes you must take a step back and realize when the cost of continuing outweighs the goal. We must always remember to put everything in perspective and think—why am I doing this? What is motivating me? Is this what I really want or am I just doing what is expected of me? By continually evaluating our actions, just as our guides did, we can all have much happier and fulfilling lives. A good leader needs to not only learn to motivate a group to persevere, but also to know when to help a group to take a step back and move in a different direction. *(Iceland)*

Vertical guide Willie Parra says, "It's not a fail not getting to the summit. The mountain's still going to be there, and you can try over and over again. It's not just about going to the summit and then back to the car." Guides have the wisdom to know that a holistic experience is as important as reaching the top of the mountain. Starting in the valley with its lush foliage, rising through wooded trails, moving through exposed scree and snow fields in the full glare of the sun, climbing above the tree line, resting until the early morning hours at high camp, outlasting sudden violent night storms, beginning the final approach to the summit before dawn breaks—to guides, these are not simply things to get through. They are an important and meaningful part of the journey. Mike Useem, a veteran of many Wharton executive and MBA treks and climbs, writes, "Thinking like the CEO or the guide does not require brilliance, but it does necessitate strategic thinking—the ability to see ahead and see the whole."[8]

Author and adventurer Sebastian Junger, writing about the colorful travels of Lewis and Clark expedition member John Colter, says:

> Life in modern society is designed to eliminate as many unforeseen events as possible, and as inviting as that seems, it leaves us hopelessly underutilized. And that is where the idea of "adventure" comes in. The word comes from the Latin *adventura*, meaning "what must happen." An adventure is a situation where the outcome is not entirely within your control. It's up to fate, in other words.[9]

Guides have learned to appreciate the journey—the adventure—as something to be savored, and the best guides do what they can to pass this wise understanding on to their summit-focused clients. "The outcome has to be unknown," says guide Wes Bunch. "Most clients start to see the big picture as it comes along—it's the journey that counts. It's far more meaningful than standing on the summit."

Life lessons abound in this area.

Participant Reflections

- I had this preconception that education is a process that takes place inside an academic institution, where a flurry of note-taking and all-nighters ensure that our grades stay as high as they can be at all costs—because failure is not an option. But this past week, the 12 of us summarily dispatched that idea. Things didn't go as planned many times in many different ways, but we dealt with the consequences and moved on—and I'm sure that if there is a next time we won't be thwarted by the same reason. We are stronger, more capable leaders with a heightened sense of awareness. I also really appreciated that we represented all six livable continents and easily at least eight languages. Together we learned about the traditions of Kenya, the castes of India, the culture of international schools in Korea—not from textbooks, but from people. That's a kind of global awareness that can't help but foster better decision-making as leaders. *(Utah)*

- Climbing the Grand was, at first, an individual challenge for me, but in a very short time, I realized that the success of the group was more important than my own. While each individual aimed to summit the mountain, I believe the group goal was to enter the challenge as a team and exit as a team. *(Grand Teton Mountaineering)*

- The entire team would probably agree that our most important lesson was learned during our summit of the glacier. We learned that although it is important to push ourselves and surge forward, it is equally if not more important to know when to stop and turn back. Although we turned back when we were only two hours away from the summit, in retrospect, not one of us would have taken a different decision. We realized, as we huddled in the van for warmth after the descent, that it really wasn't about reaching the top. We had won by trying, by enduring the worst of the weather for six hours, and by getting back down in one piece—safe, sound and together. The picture we managed to take proudly holding up the flag speaks volumes of our team. One could probably not be able to tell from our huge smiles and screams of joy that we were drenched and chilled to the bone at that moment. Our faces are definitely not those of defeat in that picture. I looked around the room as we sat around in a circle, thanking each other for the experience of a lifetime, and was surprised at how quickly I became emotional. *(Iceland)*

In Practice

Deborah Horn, who joined a Grand Teton team while a Wharton student, and is now a category manager at Microsoft, says:

> While climbing a mountain with a guide has taught me so much about myself, what it has taught me about leadership is how a guide motivates and inspires in different ways along the journey. At our night camp on the Grand Teton's Lower Saddle, the weather turned to a hard rain, and at dawn our guide delivered the message that we would have to end our summit attempt before it even began. I learned that even if the summit isn't attained, the journey is just as valuable and rewarding as standing on the peak.

Reaching the summit at work can mean a lot of things, for example, executing a successful multi-million dollar campaign that meets the metrics you established, or learning an insight about your target market that you can use as a competitive advantage. When I realized that I wasn't passionate about reaching for the same summit any longer in my day-to-day life, I found a manager at work who could see the big picture and who put me on the path for my next adventure. He helped me figure out that I wanted to investigate a totally new function in my next job, and introduced me to four other leaders across the company. One of those introductions led to a new job that has turned into a dream role and has helped me progress more quickly in my career than I thought possible.

The Message

In climbing and in life, reach as high as you can—but always keep a clear eye on the big picture. What guides teach us—*look at the big picture, enjoy the journey,* and *if you reach the summit you must still make it down safely*—has meaning far beyond the mountain trails and peaks. As the organizer of these expeditions, I was able to return time and again to the mountain—but this was not so for most. Reading again through the participants' reflections in this chapter, many of them about striving for, but not reaching, the summit, still moves me. Although the outcomes of our adventures in life are uncertain, keeping a focus on the big picture always puts things into perspective. The action steps that follow point the way.

ACTION STEPS TO SEE THE BIG PICTURE

"The more you appreciate the underlying forces that can drive success or trigger failure, and the opportunities and threats that the future may hold," Mike Useem writes, "the better you will be at decision making once your turn to lead arrives."[10] From my own observations, mountain guides are expert at recognizing systems and patterns as they ascend a peak: they know it's not just a matter of finding a safe route and having the requisite technical knowledge. From the experience of the first awkward moments of climbing school, to building a confident rope team, to the sense of wonder and awe we feel at reaching our final goal, guides can teach us much about the importance of seeing the big picture in our own lives and occupations. For a guide, the big picture is the whole system, with a honed appreciation for all its interconnected subsystems—incoming mountain weather, subtle changes in terrain and vegetation and wildlife as the team moves from subalpine to alpine environments, the ever-changing welfare of the team itself—all swirling and interacting together.

The big picture just gets bigger with the recognition that seeing the whole system is critical to the potential of our impact in society as leaders. William E. Fulmer, a former senior fellow at the Harvard Business School, writes, "Unfortunately, in the rush to introduce and embrace new concepts and practices that address new problems, we have too rarely stepped back to think about the bigger picture. Consequently, too many of us fail to see the big picture and instead focus our energies on only a part of the problem. We frequently see symptoms or problems in isolation."[11] Psychologist Daniel Goleman, in his book *Focus*, says leaders who are able to see the big picture have an "enlarged aperture." The "good-enough leader," he writes, "operates within the givens of a system to benefit a single group, executing a mission as directed, taking on the problems of the day. Great leaders do not settle for systems as they are, but see what they could become, and so work to transform them for the better, to benefit the widest circle."[12]

Consider these action steps to help you see the big picture:

- **See it as a process.**
  - Peter Senge, PhD, senior lecturer in leadership and sustainability at MIT, says that leaders should help people see the big picture. He provides some helpful suggestions for developing a big-picture view:
    - We often think about events as isolated occurrences: instead, take a broader view and look for interrelationships within a process.
    - Don't place blame on others or on outside circumstances for problems: rather, consider if the cause is actually a poorly designed system.
    - Linear thinking can encourage a hasty intervention in what is actually a complex system, making things even worse. Don't rush in with a quick fix; instead, take a systemic view and look for the underlying cause.[13]
- **Get on the balcony.**
  - Ronald Heifetz, M.D., founding director and senior lecturer at the Kennedy School's Center for Public Leadership at Harvard, says that a leader has to alternate between participating and observing. "Rather than maintain perspective on events that surround and involve us," he says, "we often get swept up by them." Heifetz likens it to the difference between being in full motion on the dance floor, where it's almost impossible to tell what's happening beyond a few feet, and being up on the balcony, where the overall patterns on the dance floor become clear.
  - For organizational leaders, though, the view from the balcony is not a retreat: Heifetz says it's a way to get the big picture before crafting a strategic response.[14]
- **Think positive.**
  - Aparna Labroo, professor of marketing at Northwestern University's Kellogg School of Management, and Vanessa Patrick, professor of marketing at the University of Houston, demonstrate that a positive mood or cue allows people to step back or distance themselves psychologically from the current situation and activates more abstract, or big-picture, thinking.[15]
  - Barbara Fredrickson, PhD, a professor of psychology and director of the positive emotions and psychophysiology laboratory at the University of North Carolina at Chapel Hill, is a leading investigator in the science of positive psychology and the life-enhancing effects of positive emotions. Negative emo-

tions and their impact on physiology (for example, fear makes us run) have been clearly linked to our adaptation and survival. But positive emotions, Fredrickson writes, "aren't so easily explained. From this evolutionary perspective, joy, serenity, and gratitude don't seem as useful as fear, anger, or disgust." Fredrickson's broaden-and-build theory suggests a different approach: instead of solving problems of immediate survival, positive emotions solve problems concerning personal growth and development. One fascinating laboratory experiment used short, emotionally evocative film clips to induce a range of emotions, from joy to sadness, in participants. Fredrickson then used a visual processing task to assess the participant's ability to think broadly by measuring whether they saw the "big picture" or focused on smaller details. She found that, compared to those in negative or neutral emotional states, participants who experience positive emotions tend to choose the global, rather than local, configuration, "suggesting a broadened pattern of thinking." Fredrickson also cites research by other investigators which demonstrates that when people feel good, their thinking becomes more creative, integrative, flexible, and open to information.[16]

- **Look into far enough into the future.**
  - Greg Shea, PhD, adjunct professor of management and a senior fellow at Wharton's Center for Leadership and Change Management, advises those charged with leading organizational change efforts to get a clear picture of the future before redesigning work systems. His suggestions:
    - Look far enough into the future to uncouple yourself from the major constraints of the present, and describe the end goal—the big picture.
    - Enhance your creative thinking by starting at a specific future moment and working back to the present to determine unique ways to reach your goals.
    - Design a bold change initiative that encourages you and your team to think system-wide, try new approaches, and develop new solutions.[17]

- **Encourage divergent thinking.**
  - Michael A. Roberto, whose analysis of the 1996 Mount Everest disaster is covered in this chapter, urges leaders to encourage organization members to speak up and make their voices heard. Leaders should:
    - Seek out information that disconfirms existing views.
    - Discourage subordinates from hiding bad news.
    - Encourage people to test critical assumptions.
    - Foster constructive dissent.
    - Ensure fair and equal opportunity for others to voice their opinions during a decision process. If flawed ideas remain unchallenged, Roberto says, creative alternatives will not be generated.
    - Recognize that multiple forces interact to affect organizational performance.
    - Consider team member views carefully and genuinely, and explain a rationale for decisions. "By doing so," Roberto writes, "leaders can encourage divergent thinking while building decision acceptance."[18]

- **Focus on the experience.**
  - Climbing "alpine style" means moving fast and light to the summit and back without carrying loads of unnecessary gear. Carl Richards, writing in the *New York Times*, says approaching life alpine style has helped him see that "what we think we need, and what we really need," are often two different things. Richards says his climb to the summit of the Grand Teton looked like it was going to be derailed by an incoming storm. "Then," he says, "I reminded myself we're having an amazing day on the mountain. The rainstorm is beautiful, and I'm with one of my best friends. What do I have to be mad about? We adjusted. We found a little shelter and enjoyed the moment. A little later, the storm passed and we moved up the mountain to see what it would give us." His focus had shifted from the singular goal of reaching the summit to a bigger yet simpler picture: appreciating the experience.[19]

ELEVEN

Leading Like a Guide

One expedition participant's experience in the workplace

How is it that those early Yosemite climbers—who never went to college and never took a business course—all formed hugely successful enterprises? There are just certain things that are crossovers from being a really good climber and being an executive. Responsibility. Courage. A tolerance for risk. And being part of a team.

—JACK TURNER

In a lot of ways, it's the perfect model for business . . .

—CHRISTIAN SANTELICES

Crossing Icelandic glaciers roped together for safety, reaching the summit of the Grand Teton in freezing temperatures, trekking remote and windblown trails surrounded by giant Himalayan peaks, exploring Patagonia's wonders—all these, and many more, were magnificent adventures and learning experiences, full of joy, surprise, companionship, and challenge at every turn.

Adventura—"what must happen"—indeed.

Above all, though, what remains most clear in my mind is what the expedition participants told me they learned from their guides and from their experiences. After all, our purpose in organizing these expeditions was to provide opportunities to learn from others whose leadership has been tested, to learn from experience in making decisions and leading teams in new and unfamiliar surroundings, and to productively apply that knowledge in new situations. To this end, I have included many excerpts from participants' reflections throughout the book. As I close *Lead Like a Guide,* I want to include one more, slightly longer, note that I received from a participant, Sarah Skye Gilbert, who wrote to me some years after her guide-led expedition.

Gilbert, who in addition to her degree in economics from Wharton simultaneously earned two more undergraduate degrees from the University of Pennsylvania (and later, a global executive MBA from INSEAD), joined a guided Grand Teton climbing venture as an undergraduate. A storm prevented her team from reaching the summit, but her willingness to continue to seek out stretch experiences is evident from both her academic and professional trajectories. A world traveler, Gilbert has lived in China and spent seven months conducting psychology research in Senegal, West Africa. Her amateur mountaineering career has included guided climbs of Mount Kinabalu (Borneo), Mont Blanc (Alps), and Mount Meru (Tanzania), as well as many unguided climbs in Washington and British Columbia.

Gilbert worked as an associate at The Boston Consulting Group after graduation, where she spent the majority of her time as a consultant to the Gates Foundation. She now works as a program officer on the vaccine delivery team for the Bill and Melinda Gates Foundation's global development program, based in Seattle, where she focuses on improving the quality, availability, and use of immunization data to inform decision making at all levels of the health system.

Here, Gilbert offers some thoughts on applying several of the leadership strengths of world-class guides—adapting her leadership style to fit the situation, managing risk, and applying skills in social intelligence to build strong and positive relationships—as she interacts with multiple organizations involved in improving global health.

First, guides are expert in leading flexibly, changing their style to best match the strengths of their clients and as environmental conditions warrant. Gilbert finds similarities in her own work at the Gates Foundation:

> In managing grants, I have to use very different leadership styles with different grantees. Some have strong capabilities, are fully aligned with our organization's mission, and share our risk appetite. In those cases my role is to make the grant-making process as streamlined as possible, ensure that

Skye Gilbert. (Photo courtesy of Skye Gilbert)

grantees have access to all the information that comes across my desk, and publicize their work to other development partners and countries, in case there is interest in expanding it.

Other grantees may be more risk-averse than our organization, or still in the process of building capabilities. In these cases, I either provide or pull in others who can advise on capability building. I also continuously demonstrate my comfort with them taking risks, which requires more interactions and real clarity on both the grant-making process and the Gates Foundation's definition of success. For example, if I want the grantee to be making data-driven decisions rather than instinctual ones, and be comfortable with failure, I need to model that by consistently refusing to accept instinct-based decisions, even when I agree with them, unless data supports the decision. I also have to be prepared to publicly change my mind and acknowledge that I was wrong if new information does not support my previous perspective.

Second, guides manage risk and uncertainty at every turn. Here, Gilbert talks about a risk that many of us face in the workplace—*burnout*—and how she learned to manage it:

In the mountains, turning away from a summit can be hard, but when the risk to a climber's safety is too high, a wise guide will make the decision to turn around. In a mission-driven organization like the Gates Foundation, people set tough goals and aim high, and the risk of burnout here is even higher than in industries such as banking or consulting. This is because on top of feeling the need to prove yourself through hard work and being fully engaged in what you're doing, you also feel the weight of the world on your shoulders. When I arrived at the organization I was told, "Spend these millions of dollars as optimally as you can to improve health information systems for immunization programs in Africa, so these programs can reach more kids and prevent epidemics like measles."

Well, information systems have a lot of different end users, from the nurse who uses the data to track children who miss hospital visits, to Bill and Melinda Gates, who use the data to make powerful decisions about what to invest in, and where. Designing a system that meets all needs across numerous stakeholders poses a real challenge. The volume of information related to my work is overwhelming—you can spend a lifetime just going through all the relevant articles and talking to people with experience in order to inform how you invest, so there's a lot to learn from and build on. You can feel that if you don't work constantly, you're letting someone, somewhere in the world down.

As I prepared my annual holiday letter this year, I placed photos of my work life next to my personal life and felt guilty about the pictures of me with friends or on a mountain. I felt like in each of those moments I was abandoning the mission to go play. But I've now come to realize that eradicating diseases and saving lives is a long-term game, and it's probably not in our industry's best interest to have people rotate in, work hard for two years, and then leave and take all their experience and knowledge with them when they burn out. It's far better to give myself and my team permission to restore. I've since been instilling the importance of time off into my team by telling them not to work on weekends, to build time into their work day for reflection, and asking them about, and valuing, what they do in their free time. I think in this way we'll be together and strong for the next summit.

Finally, Gilbert relates what social intelligence means to her in her work environment:

We have multiple investments in building peer-to-peer networks between country governments. These networks connect via in-person meetings, webinars, Google Groups emails, blogs, discussion threads, and, more recently, WhatsApp. In the early days of some of these networks, I observed that participants from some countries tended to be quieter, while technical partners from NGOs, UN organizations, and donor organizations, including ours, were dominating a lot of the exchanges. We've since been experimenting with different strategies to change that balance.

Where we've been successful in increasing country exchanges and reducing the dominance of technical partners, it's been due to some investigation of why people didn't want to respond to an email chain or ask a question, then methodically removing barriers that were identified. Most of the barriers were "soft" and involved cultural norms and power dynamics, and our changes involved softening language, redoing agendas so there was explicit time dedicated to quieter participants offering their thoughts, and even by removing high-powered people from some conversations (for example, more frank discussions can happen if a donor isn't in the room). We also offered behind-the-scenes coaching for people who had critical things to say but needed confidence to hit the 'send' button. Our hope is that some of the insights gained from embedding social intelligence within the management of these peer networks will lead to stronger, sustained networks and, over time, help shift the balance of voice away from global partners and more towards local implementers.

Now, take a moment to visualize the impact of leading like a guide in your own workplace. Take stock of the benefits of building and maintaining positive relationships as you travel the peaks and valleys of business strategy or the nonprofit funding cycle, and the advantage of being able to switch smoothly between leadership styles when conditions demand it. Consider how engaged your colleagues will feel when they are encouraged and empowered to innovate, make decisions, and take action, and what it would be like to actively build trusting relationships that encourage others to take that first, scary step forward into new territory. Imagine encouraging initiative and entrepreneurial action while still remaining risk aware in an environment of constant flux and uncertainty, and keeping the big picture of your enterprise in mind as you strive to reach your target without falling victim to blind ambition—what mountaineers know all too well as "summit fever."

I believe that the six leadership strengths of world-class mountain guides hold great promise for leaders who choose to apply them in their chosen occupations and in life.

Lead like a guide!

Notes

PREFACE

1. Maxwell, C. "Believing Is Seeing: A Mountaineer Talks to Business About Overcoming Adversity." *Wharton Leadership Digest* 10, no. 7 (April, 2006): http://www.leadlikeaguide.com/resources/believing/

2. Turner, J. "Trust" (presentation to Wharton School Grand Teton Mountaineering participants, Grand Teton Climbers' Ranch, Grand Teton National Park, Wyoming. August 17, 2004).

3. Lhotse Case 2006. Courtesy of Vertical S.A., and the Wharton School of the University of Pennsylvania.

4. Bernbaum, E. "Lessons from the Top: Mount Fuji, Mount Sinai, and Other Peak Paradigms." In *Upward Bound: Nine Original Accounts of How Business Leaders Reached Their Summits,* ed. Useem, M., Useem, J., & Asel, P. (New York: Crown Business, 2003): 168–185.

5. Pfeffer, J. *Leadership BS: Fixing Workplaces and Careers One Truth at a Time.* (New York: Harper Business, 2015): 50.

6. Useem, M. "The Leadership Lessons of Mount Everest." *Harvard Business Review* 79, no. 9 (2001): 51–58.

7. Wharton Leadership Ventures offers Wharton students *workshops* (seminar-style, one-day), *intensives* (one- or two-day experiences, low to medium in physical intensity), and *expeditions* (6–14 day expeditions, high in physical intensity). *See* https://leadership.wharton.upenn.edu

8. Fedarko, K. "The House of Rock." *Outside* (April 2004): 70–80, 121.

9. Fowler, J.H., & Christakis, N.A. "Dynamic Spread of Happiness in a Large Social Network: Longitudinal Analysis of the Framingham Heart Study Social Network." *British Medical Journal* 338 (January 3, 2009): 23–27. http://www.bmj.com/content/337/bmj.a2338

10. Fowler, J.H., & Christakis, N.A. "Cooperative Behavior Cascades in Human Social Networks." *PNAS* 107, no. 12 (2010): 5334–5338.

11. Christakis, N.A., & Fowler, J.H. *Connected: The Surprising Power of Our Social Networks and How They Shape Our Lives.* (New York: Little Brown, 2009): xi.

CHAPTER 1

1. Prospectus for *Wharton Leadership Trek to Mt. Everest,* May 2–18, 2001, organized by Edwin Bernbaum and Michael Useem.

2. Useem, M. "The Leadership Lessons of Mount Everest." *Harvard Business Review* 79, no. 9 (2001): 51–58.

3. Ibid.

4. Preston Cline, e-mail message to author, November 9, 2015.

5. *See*, Useem, M. *The Leader's Checklist.* (Philadelphia: Wharton Digital Press, 2011).

6. Gurdjian, P., Halbeisen, T., Lane, K. "Why Leadership-Development Programs Fail." *McKinsey Quarterly* (January 2014): http://www.mckinsey.com/insights /leading_in_the_21st_century/why_leadership-development_programs_fail

7. Kolb, A.Y., & Kolb, D.A. "Learning Styles and Learning Spaces: Enhancing Experiential Education in Higher Education." *Academy of Management Learning & Education* 4, no. 2 (2005): 193–212.

8. Useem, M., Davidson, M., & Wittenberg, E. "Leadership Development Beyond the Classroom: The Value of Leadership Ventures to Instruct Leadership Decision Making." *International Journal of Leadership Education* 1 (2005): 159–178.

9. Kolb, A. Y., & Kolb, D.A., op. cit.

10. Holmes, J. *Nonsense: The Power of Not Knowing.* (New York: Crown Publishers, 2015): 9–10.

11. Ibid., 11.

12. Useem, M., Davidson, M., & Wittenberg, E., op. cit.

13. Darling, M., Parry, C., & Moore, J. "Learning in the Thick of It." *Harvard Business Review* 83, no. 7 (2005): 84–92, 192.

14. Headquarters, Department of the Army. "A Leader's Guide to After-Action Reviews." Training Circular 25-20 (September 30, 1993): http://www.acq.osd.mil /dpap/ccap/cc/jcchb/Files/Topical/After_Action_Report/resources/tc25-20.pdf

15. Henshaw, T. "After-Action Reviews." *Nano Tools for Leaders* (April 2012): http://executiveeducation.wharton.upenn.edu/thought-leadership/wharton-at -work/2012/04/after-action-reviews

16. Useem, M., Davidson, M., & Wittenberg, E., op. cit.

CHAPTER 2

1. Useem, M. "Mt. Everest, Part II: Learning from a Second Climb of the World's Highest Mountain." *Knowledge@Wharton* (April 9, 2012): http://knowledge .wharton.upenn.edu/article/mt-everest-part-ii-learning-from-a-second-climb-of -the-worlds-highest-mountain/

2. Rodrigo Jordan in discussion with the author, June 21, 2016.

3. Jordan, R., & Garay, M. *Experiential Leadership: From Principles to Practice.* 2d. ed. (Santiago, Chile: Vertical, S.A., 2014), 191–199.

4. Ibid., 172, 193, 204–205.

5. Jordan, R. *Expeditions to the Heart of Climate Change: Antarctica/Greenland.* (Santiago, Chile: Fundación Vertical/Recalcine, 2008): 113.

CHAPTER 3

1. Turiano, T. *Selected Peaks of Greater Yellowstone.* (Jackson, WY: Indomitus Books, 2003): 395–430.

2. Jackson, R.G. "Park of the Matterhorns." *Grand Teton Historic Resource Study.* (Washington, DC: National Park Service, 2004). http://www.nps.gov/park history/online_books/grte2/hrs16.htm

3. Ibid.

4. Ibid.

5. Absolon, M. "Paul Tells His Story." *The Leader* (Fall 1995): http://www.nols .edu/alumni/leader/95fall/paultellshisstory.shtml

6. Craighead, C., ed. *Glenn Exum: Never a Bad Word or a Twisted Rope. A Collection of Climbing Stories by Glenn Exum.* (Moose, WY: Grand Teton Natural History Association, 1998): 3.

7. Read, A. "First Mover Advantage: Tenacity and the Business of Adventure." In *Upward Bound: Nine Original Accounts of How Business Leaders Reached Their Summits,* ed. Useem, M., Useem, J., & Asel, P. (New York: Crown Business, 2003): 186–204.

8. "Twenty Classics in Twenty Days (from California to Wyoming)." *American Alpine Journal* 36, no. 68 (1994): 141.

CHAPTER 4

1. Breemer, C. "Taste the Paine: Twenty Days on a Patagonian Mega-Route." *Climbing* (August 1—September 15, 1995): 80–87, 159–161.

2. Breemer, C. "Escudo, East Face, Paine Group." *American Alpine Journal* 69, no. 37 (1995): 221–222.

3. Interviews with Christian Santelices: December 27, 2005 (Jackson, WY); March 22, 2007 (Philadelphia); March 10, 2014 (Needles Outpost, UT); May 15, 2014 (Philadelphia).

4. Lambert, E. "Turner Endures: First Grade VII Solo." *Alpinist (Newswire)* (February 4, 2008): http://www.alpinist.com/doc/web07-08w/newswire-dave -turner-patagonia-solo-vii

CHAPTER 5

1. Goleman, D. *Emotional Intelligence.* (New York, Bantam Books, 1995): 14.

2. Salovey, P., & Mayer, J.D. "Emotional Intelligence." *Imagination, Cognition and Personality* 9 (1990): 185–211.

3. Barsade, S.G., & Gibson, D.E. "Why Does Affect Matter in Organizations?" *Academy of Management Perspectives* 21 (2005): 36–59.

4. Thorndike, E.L. "Intelligence and Its Use." *Harper's Magazine* 140 (1920): 227–235.

5. Peterson, C., & Seligman, M.E.P. *Character Strengths and Virtues: A Handbook and Classification.* (New York: Oxford University Press and Washington, DC: American Psychological Association, 2004): 338–339.

6. Ibid.

7. Interview with Rodrigo Jordan. "Tackling Poverty and Climbing Mountains, in Chile and Beyond." *Knowledge@Wharton* (January 10, 2007): http://knowledge .wharton.upenn.edu/article/tackling-poverty-and-climbing-mountains-in-chile -and-beyond/

8. Petzoldt, P. *The Wilderness Handbook.* (New York: W.W. Norton, 1974): 127–143.

9. Harvey, M. *The National Outdoor Leadership School's Wilderness Guide.* (New York: Fireside Books, 1999): 165–177.

10. Kanengieter, J., & Rajagopal-Durbin, A. "Wilderness Leadership—On the Job." *Harvard Business Review* 90, no. 4 (2012): 127–131.

11. Goleman, D. *Social Intelligence: The New Science of Human Relationships.* (New York: Bantam Dell, 2006): 11–12.

12. Goleman, D., & Boyatzis, R. "Social Intelligence and the Biology of Leadership." *Harvard Business Review* 86, no. 9 (2008): 74–81.

13. Ibid.

14. Goleman (2006), op. cit., 84.

15. Goldsmith, M. "The One Skill That Separates." *Fast Company* 96 (July 2005): 86. http://www.fastcompany.com/53175/skill-separates

16. Gable, S.L., Reis, H.T., Impett, E.A., & Asher, E.R. "What Do You Do When Things Go Right? The Intrapersonal and Interpersonal Benefits of Sharing Positive Events." *Journal of Personality and Social Psychology* 87, no. 2 (2004): 228–245.

17. McQuaid, M., & Lawn, E. *Your Strengths Blueprint: How to Be Engaged, Energized, and Happy at Work.* (Albert Park, Victoria, Australia: McQuaid Pty. Ltd., 2014).

18. Halvorson, H.G. "3 Ways to Project Warmth and Trustworthiness." (March 26, 2015): http://www.fastcompany.com/3044285/work-smart/3-ways-to -project-warmth-and-trustworthiness

19. Kleiner, A. "Thomas Malone on Building Smarter Teams." *strategy+business* (May 12, 2014): http://www.strategy-business.com/article/00257. See *also* Woolley, A., Malone, T.W., & Chabris, C.F. "Why Some Teams Are Smarter than Others." *The New York Times Sunday Review* (January 16, 2015): http://www .nytimes.com/2015/01/18/opinion/sunday/why-some-teams-are-smarter-than -others.html

20. "Why Fostering an Environment of 'Compassionate Love' in the Workplace Matters." *Knowledge@Wharton* (April 2, 2014): http://knowledge.wharton.upenn .edu/article/fostering-culture-compassion-workplace-matters/

CHAPTER 6

1. Goleman, D. "Leadership That Gets Results." *Harvard Business Review* 78, no. 2 (2000): 78–90.

2. Rébuffat, G. *Starlight and Storm: The Conquest of the Great North Faces of the Alps.* (New York: Modern Library, [1956] 1999): 196.

3. Goleman, op. cit.

4. Useem, M. "Mt. Everest, Part II: Learning from a Second Climb of the World's Highest Mountain." *Knowledge@Wharton* (April 9, 2012): http://knowledge .wharton.upenn.edu/article/mt-everest-part-ii-learning-from-a-second-climb-of -the-worlds-highest-mountain/

5. Ones, D.S., & Dilchert, S. "How Special are Executives? How Special Should Executive Selection Be? Observations and Recommendations." *Industrial and Organizational Psychology* 2, no. 2 (2009): 163–170.

6. Grant, A.M., Gino, F., & Hofmann, D.A. "The Hidden Advantages of Quiet Bosses." *Harvard Business Review* 88, no. 12 (2010): 28.

7. Grant, A.M., Gino, F., & Hofmann, D.A. "Stop Stealing the Spotlight: The Perils of Extraverted Leadership." *European Business Review* (May-June, 2011): 29–31. *See also* Grant, A.M., Gino, F., & Hofmann, D.A. "Reversing the Extra-verted Leadership Advantage: The Role of Employee Proactivity." *Academy of Management Journal* 54, no. 3 (2011): 528–550.

8. Cain, S. *Quiet: The Power of Introverts in a World That Can't Stop Talking.* (New York: Crown): 53.

9. Bernstein, E. "Why Introverts Make Great Entrepreneurs." *Wall Street Journal* (August 24, 2015): http://www.wsj.com/articles/why-introverts-make-great -entrepreneurs-1440381699

10. Grant et al., *European Business Review,* op. cit. *See also* "Analyzing Effective Leaders: Why Extraverts Are Not Always the Most Successful Bosses." *Knowledge@Wharton* (November 23, 2010): http://knowledge.wharton.upenn.edu/article /analyzing-effective-leaders-why-extraverts-are-not-always-the-most-successful -bosses/

11. Sharer, K. "How Should Your Leaders Behave?" *Harvard Business Review* 91, no. 10 (2013): 40. https://hbr.org/2013/10/how-should-your-leaders-behave

12. Ibid.

13. Goleman, op. cit.

14. Senge, P. "The Leader's New Work: Building Learning Organizations." *Sloan Management Review* 32, no. 1 (1990): 7–23.

15. Grant, A. *Give and Take: A Revolutionary Approach to Success.* (New York: Viking, 2013): 61–93.

16. Edmondson, A. "Psychological Safety and Learning Behavior in Work Teams." *Administrative Science Quarterly* 44, no. 2 (1999): 350–383.

17. McChrystal, S. *Team of Teams: New Rules of Engagement for a Complex World.* (New York: Portfolio/Penguin, 2015): 220–232.

CHAPTER 7

1. Hassan, S., Mahsud, R., Yukl, G., & Prussia, G.E. "Ethical and Empowering Leadership and Leadership Effectiveness." *Journal of Managerial Psychology* 28, no. 2 (2013): 133–146.

2. Arnold, J.A., Arad, S., Rhoades, J.A., & Drasgow, F. "The Empowering Leadership Questionnaire: The Construction and Validation of a New Scale for Measuring Leader Behaviors." *Journal of Organizational Behavior* 21, no. 3 (2000): 249–269.

3. Grant, A. *Give and Take: A Revolutionary Approach to Success.* (New York: Viking, 2013): 4.

4. Lorinkova, N.M., Pearsall, M.J., & Sims, H.P. "Examining the Differential Longitudinal Performance of Directive versus Empowering Leadership in Teams." *Academy of Management Journal* 56, no. 2 (2013): 573–596.

5. Quinn, R.E., & Spreitzer, G.M. "The Road to Empowerment: Seven Questions Every Leader Should Consider." *Organizational Dynamics* 26, no. 2 (Autumn, 1997): 37–49.

6. Spreitzer, G. 2007. "Taking Stock: A Review of More than Twenty Years of Research on Empowerment at Work." In *The Handbook of Organizational Behavior,* edited by C. Cooper and J. Barling. (Thousand Oaks, CA: Sage Publications, 2007): 54–73.

7. Schaufeli, W.B., & Bakker, A.B. "Job Demands, Job Resources, and their Relationship with Burnout and Engagement: A Multi-Sample Study." *Journal of Organizational Behavior* 25, no. 3 (2004): 293–315.

8. Schwartz, T., & Porath, C. "Why You Hate Work." *New York Times* (May 30, 2014): http://www.nytimes.com/2014/06/01/opinion/sunday/why-you-hate-work .html

9. Quiñones, M., Van den Broeck, A., & De Witte, H. "Do Job Resources Affect Work Engagement via Psychological Empowerment? A Mediation Analysis." *Journal of Work and Organizational Psychology* 29 (2013): 127–134.

10. Schwartz & Porath, op. cit.

11. George, B. "Fixing the 'I Hate Work' Blues." *Harvard Business School Working Knowledge* (June 5, 2014): http://hbswk.hbs.edu/item/fixing-the-i-hate-work -blues

12. Ibarra, H. *Act Like a Leader, Think Like a Leader.* (Boston: Harvard Business Review Press, 2015): 25–69.

13. Useem, M. *The Leadership Moment: Nine True Stories of Triumph and Disaster and Their Lessons for Us All.* (New York: Times Books, 1998): 270–271.

14. Ancona, D., & Bresman, H. *X-Teams: How to Build Teams That Lead, Innovate, and Succeed.* (Boston: Harvard Business School Press, 2007): 230–232.

15. Kotter, J.P., and Cohen, D.S. *The Heart of Change: Real-Life Stories of How People Change their Organizations.* (Boston: Harvard Business Review Press, 2002): 101–121.

16. Kotter, J.P. 1996. *Leading Change.* (Boston: Harvard Business School Press, Boston, 1996): 101–115.

17. Grant, A.M., Campbell, E.M., Chen, G., Cottone, K., Lapedis, D., & Lee, K. "Impact and the Art of Motivation Maintenance: The Effects of Contact with Beneficiaries on Persistence Behavior." *Organizational Behavior and Human Decision Processes* 103 (2007): 53–67.

18. Grant, A.M. "How Customers Can Rally Your Troops: End Users Can Energize Your Workforce Far Better Than Your Managers Can." *Harvard Business Review* (June, 2011): 98–103.

19. "Employee Engagement: Making a Difference." *Wharton@Work NanoTools for Leaders* (May 2015): http://executiveeducation.wharton.upenn.edu/thought-leadership/wharton-at-work/2015/05/employee-engagement

CHAPTER 8

1. Mayer, R.C., Davis, J.H., & Schoorman, F.D. "An Integrative Model of Organizational Trust." *Academy of Management Review* 20, no. 3 (1995): 709–734.

2. Ibid.

3. Jordan, R. "Strategy at the Crux." In *Upward Bound: Nine Original Accounts of How Business Leaders Reached Their Summits,* ed. Useem, M., Useem, J., & Asel, P. (New York: Crown Business, 2003): 158–159.

4. Ibid.

5. Giddens, A. *The Consequences of Modernity.* (Stanford, CA: Stanford University Press, 1990): 33.

6. Ibid.

7. Ibid.

8. Franklin, B. *The Autobiography of Benjamin Franklin.* Labaree, L.W., Ketcham, R.L., Boatfield, H.C., & Fineman, H.H., eds. (New Haven: Yale University Press, 1964): 148–150.

9. Peterson, C., & Seligman, M.E.P. *Character Strengths and Virtues: A Handbook and Classification.* (New York: Oxford University Press and Washington, DC: American Psychological Association, 2004).

10. *See VIA Survey of Character*: https://www.viasurvey.org

11. Simpson, J.A. "Psychological Foundations of Trust." *Current Directions in Psychological Science* 16 (2007): 264–268.

12. Shell, G.R. *Bargaining for Advantage: Negotiation Strategies for Reasonable People.* (New York: Penguin Books, 2000): 68–70, 137.

13. Ibid., 69.

14. Shell, G.R., & Moussa, M. *The Art of Woo: Using Strategic Persuasion to Sell Your Ideas.* (New York: Penguin Books, 2007): 85–109.

15. Pandola, T., & Bird, J.W. *Light a Fire under Your Business: How to Build a Class 1 Corporate Structure through Inspirational Leadership.* (Santa Barbara, CA: Praeger, 2015): 78–80.

16. Cuddy, A.J.C., Kohut, M., & Neffinger, J. "Connect, Then Lead." *Harvard Business Review* 91, nos. 7/8 (2013): 54–61.

17. Javetsky, B. "Leading in the 21st Century: An Interview with Michael Useem." *McKinsey & Company, Insights and Publications* (September, 2012): http://www.mckinsey.com/insights/leading_in_the_21st_century/an_interview_with_michael_useem

18. DeSteno, D. *The Truth About Trust: How It Determines Success in Life, Love, Learning, and More.* (New York: Hudson Street Press, 2014): 22–26.

19. Ibid., 162.

20. DeSteno, D. "Who Can You Trust?" *Harvard Business Review* 92, no. 3 (2014): 112–115.

21. DeSteno, D. *The Truth About Trust: How It Determines Success in Life, Love, Learning, and More.* (New York: Hudson Street Press, 2014): 170–172.

CHAPTER 9

1. Maxwell, C., & Read, A. "Leadership at the Sharp End of the Rope: Guiding Guides." *Wharton Leadership Digest* 11, no. 2 (November, 2006): http://www.leadlikeaguide.com/resources/leadership/

2. Lipshitz, R., & Strauss, O. "Coping with Uncertainty: A Naturalistic Decision-Making Analysis." *Organizational Behavior and Human Decision Processes* 69, no. 2 (1997): 149–163.

3. Asel, P. "Scaling Up: Ridge Walking from Silicon Valley to McKinley's Summit." In *Upward Bound: Nine Original Accounts of How Business Leaders Reached Their Summits*, Useem, M., Useem, J, & Asel, P. (New York: Crown Business, 2003): 119.

4. Lyng, S. "Edgework: A Social and Psychological Analysis of Voluntary Risk-Taking." *The American Journal of Sociology* 95, no. 4 (1990): 851–886.

5. Ibid.

6. Ebert, P., & Robertson, S. "A Plea for Risk." *Royal Institute of Philosophy Supplement* 73 (2013): 45–64.

7. Ibid.

8. Rébuffat, G. *Starlight and Storm: The Conquest of the Great North Faces of the Alps.* (New York: Modern Library, [1956] 1999): xlv.

9. Giddens, A. *The Consequences of Modernity.* (Stanford, CA: Stanford University Press, 1990): 21–28.

10. Maxwell, C. "Uncertainty and Trust: Leadership Lessons at High Altitude." *Wharton Leadership Digest* 9, no. 1 (October, 2004): http://www.leadlikeaguide.com/resources/uncertainty/

11. Giddens, op. cit. 28–30.

12. Kahneman, D. *Thinking, Fast and Slow.* (New York: Farrar, Straus and Giroux, 2011): 282–283.

13. Bremmer, I. "Managing Risk in an Unstable World." *Harvard Business Review* 83, no. 6 (2005): 51–60.

14. Kunreuther, H., & Useem, M. "Principles and Challenges for Reducing Risks from Disasters." In *Learning from Catastrophes: Strategies for Reaction and*

Response, ed. Kunreuther, H., & Useem, M. (Upper Saddle River, NJ: Wharton School Publishing, 2009): 1–17.

15. Maxwell, C. "Hospital Organizational Response to the Nuclear Accident at Three Mile Island: Implications for Future-Oriented Disaster Planning." *American Journal of Public Health* 72, no. 3 (1982): 275–279.

16. Gawande, A. *The Checklist Manifesto: How to Get Things Right.* (New York: Metropolitan Books, 2009).

17. Ibid.

18. Boyd, E.B. "4 Rules for Managing from a Decorated Force Recon Marine." *Fast Company* (October 29, 2013): http://www.fastcompany.com/3020714/innovation-agents/4-rules-for-managing-risk-from-a-decorated-force-recon-marine

19. Useem, M. *The Leader's Checklist,* 2nd ed. (Philadelphia: Wharton Digital Press, 2011).

20. Kanengieter, J., & Rajagopal-Durbin, A. "Wilderness Leadership—On the Job: Five Principles from Outdoor Exploration That Will Make You a Better Manager." *Harvard Business Review* 90, no. 4 (2012): 127–131, 147.

21. Kolditz, T. *In Extremis Leadership: Leading as if Your Life Depended on It.* (San Francisco: Jossey-Bass, 2007): 5–7, 85–90.

22. Rébuffat, G. *Starlight and Storm: The Conquest of the Great North Faces of the Alps.* (New York: Modern Library, [1956] 1999): 186–187.

23. Graydon, D., & Hanson, G. (eds.) 1997. *Mountaineering: The Freedom of the Hills.* 6th ed. (Seattle: The Mountaineers, 1997): 442–446.

CHAPTER 10

1. Breemer, C. "Taste the Paine: Twenty Days on a Patagonian Mega-Route." *Climbing* (August 1—September 15, 1995): 80–87, 159–161.

2. Venables, S. "Mt. Everest: The View from the Top." *The Guardian* (May 29, 2013): http://www.theguardian.com/world/2013/may/29/mount-everest-view-from-top

3. Firth, P.G., Zheng, H., Windsor, J.S., Sutherland, A.I., Imray, C.H., Moore, G.W.K., Semple, J.L., Roach, R.C., & Salisbury, R.A. "Mortality on Mount Everest, 1921–2006: Descriptive Study." *British Medical Journal* (Dec. 11, 2008): 337:a2654.

4. Krakauer, J. *Into Thin Air.* (New York: Villard, 1999).

5. Roberto, M.A. "Lessons from Everest: The Interaction of Cognitive Bias, Psychological Safety, and System Complexity." *California Management Review* 45, no. 1 (2002): 136–158.

6. Ibid.

7. Ibid.

8. Useem, M. "Thinking Like a Guide." In *Upward Bound: Nine Original Accounts of How Business Leaders Reached Their Summits,* ed. Useem, M., Useem, J, & Asel, P. (New York: Crown Business, 2003): 206.

9. Junger, S. "Colter's Way." In *Fire.* (New York: Harper Collins, 2002): 150.

10. Useem, op. cit., 205–223.

11. Fulmer, W.E. *Shaping the Adaptive Organization: Landscapes, Learning, and Leadership in Volatile Times.* (New York: AMACOM, 2000): 21.

12. Goleman, D. *Focus: The Hidden Driver of Excellence.* (New York: Harper-Collins, 2013): 254–255.

13. Senge, P.M. "The Leader's New Work: Building Learning Organizations." *Sloan Management Review* 32, no. 1 (1990): 7–23.

14. Heifetz, R.A. *Leadership Without Easy Answers.* (Cambridge, MA: The Belknap Press, 1994): 250–276.

15. Labroo, A.A., & Patrick, V.M. "Psychological Distancing: Why Happiness Helps You See the Big Picture." *Journal of Consumer Research* 35, no. 5 (2009): 800–809.

16. Fredrickson, B.L. "The Value of Positive Emotions." *American Scientist* 91, no. 4 (2003): 330–335.

17. Shea, G.P., & Solomon, C.A. *Leading Successful Change: Eight Keys to Making Change Work.* (Philadelphia: Wharton Digital Press, 2013): 21.

18. Roberto, op. cit.

19. Richards, C. "What Mountain Climbing Can Teach You About Business." *New York Times* (June 15, 2015): http://www.nytimes.com/2015/06/15/your-money/what-mountain-climbing-can-teach-you-about-business.html

Index

About the Guides

(Guide service affiliation at the time of interview is in parentheses.)

Gabriel Becker (Vertical)

Gabriel has been mountaineering and climbing since he was 13 years old, and is qualified as a Chilean mountain guide. He has participated in numerous expeditions in the northern and central Andes, and in Patagonia. In addition, he has participated in scientific and commercial expeditions to the Chilean South Patagonian ice fields, Mount Kilimanjaro in Africa, Mount Fansipan in Vietnam, and Mount Ararat in Turkey, as well as high-altitude treks in Bhutan, to Mount Everest Base Camp, and in the Antarctic Peninsula. He previously worked as a logistics manager for an expedition air cruise company. He is general coordinator of expeditions and logistics for Vertical, where he supports programs of adventure education and social skills development with national and international companies and universities. Gabriel reached the summits of Lhotse in 2006 and Mount Everest in 2012.

Rodrigo Jordan Fuchs (Vertical)

Rodrigo Jordan is the founder and chairman of Vertical, S.A., an organization focused on experiential leadership education, based in Santiago, Chile. He holds a PhD in innovation from Oxford University and a graduate degree in civil industrial engineering from the Pontifical Catholic University of Chile (PUC). Jordan is widely recognized in Latin America for his work in leadership and innovation. He is the author of *Leadership: From Theory to Practice* (Spanish, Prentice-Hall 2008) and is the host of "Leadership in Person," a TV show for Chile's Canal 13, interviewing Chile's most important leaders. In addition, he serves as professor of leadership in the MBA program at the PUC School of Business. In both 2000 and 2008, he was invited to serve as a judge for the distinguished Rolex Awards for Enterprise. Jordan regularly runs seminars on leadership and the development of high-performance teams to a wide variety of clients throughout Latin America and beyond, including extensive work with the Wharton Leadership Ventures program.

Jordan, who reached the summit of Mount Everest with Vertical teams in 1992, 2012, and 2016, is considered one of Chile's most accomplished mountaineers, having led several successful expeditions to the Himalayas and Antarctica, including Everest, K2, and Mount Lhotse, the fourth-highest mountain in the world, where he led a team of 15 to the summit in 2006. In 2008, he participated in two important expeditions to Antarctica (with National Geographic and Explorers Club) and Greenland to document the impact of climate change on the world's glacial masses. Jordan has authored a number of books and documentaries based on these expeditions, including *Everest: The Challenge of a Dream; K2: The Ultimate Challenge; Planet Antarctica;* and *One Day in Chile.*

Jordan also directs Fundación Vertical, the not-for-profit arm of Vertical, which serves underprivileged students from the poorest schools in Chile, as well as promoting the enjoyment, responsible use and conservation of the environment. In 2004, he received the highest honor given by the Chilean Ministry of Education—the Order of Gabriela Mistral—for his contribution to Chilean education, and in 2008, he was the first non-American to be honored with the Gilbert M. Grosvenor Medal (named after a president of the board of National Geographic) for contributions to both education and geography.

Eugenio "Kiko" Guzmán (Vertical)

Kilo Guzmán was trained as an agricultural engineer at the Pontifical Catholic University of Chile. In 2002, Kiko was a member of the Chilean Antarctic Expedition, the first unsupported crossing of the Ellsworth Mountains Range. In 2004, and again in 2012, he reached the summit of Mount Everest. In 2005 he climbed Alaska's Denali and Indonesia's Carstenz Pyramid. In 2006 he climbed Lhotse, the world's fourth highest mountain. In 2008 Kiko participated in an expedition to Greenland to study the impact of climate change on the country's glaciers. Currently, he is the general manager of Vertical Expeditions, as well as senior lecturer at Instituto Vertical.

Guillermo "Willie" Parra (Vertical)

Willie Parra studied ecotourism at Andrés Bello University, Santiago, Chile. He is a naturalist, mountaineer, PADI dive master, and photographer. Willie has climbed mountains in Chile, Bolivia, and Argentina, including Aconcagua, the highest mountain in the western hemisphere. At Vertical since 2004, he is a guide and logistics planner for expeditions in Antarctica, Patagonia, and the Atacama Desert. From 2010 to 2012 he was part of a four-person team in a high-altitude archeological project, documenting Inca ritual sites in the north of Chile through digital video and photography, in partnership with the Chilean Pre-Columbian Art Museum and the National Geographic Society. He has also worked as explorations manager for the Explora Hotels in Torres del Paine National Park, Easter Island,

and the Atacama Desert. He served as guide and base camp manager for Vertical's 2014 Mount Everest expedition.

Fernando Yañez (Vertical)

Fernando Yañez holds a BS in agricultural science from the University of Chile. In addition to guiding for Vertical, Fernando is an entrepreneur who runs his own consulting business, dedicated to the agribusiness industry. He and his team started and operate an olive oil farm that had its first harvest during the 2014 season. He has been involved in outdoor activities since he was a teenager, pursuing mountaineering and climbing since his college years. He has worked for more than 10 years as a guide and facilitator with Vertical.

Wesley Bunch (Exum)

Wes has been a guide for 23 years, with rock climbs throughout the United States, Canada, Mexico, and Greece, including big walls in Yosemite and Zion National Parks. He has completed over 400 ascents of the Grand Teton. His ski exploits include major ski traverses of many ranges within the United States, including numerous remote traverses of the Yellowstone Ecosystem, and steep ski descents in the United States, Canada, France, and Chile. Wes was an early pioneer of steep skiing instruction and guiding in the United States and abroad, including ski expeditions to Mount Rainier and numerous high peaks in the Andes, and an expedition to ski Cho Oyu, Tibetan Himalaya. His other expeditions include Broad Peak, Karakoram Range, Pakistan; an expedition to Mount Jambeyang, China; and an exploratory expedition to Chilean Patagonia. He has made 15 ascents of Denali and 30 ascents of Aconcagua.

Amy Carse (Exum)

Between 1994 and 2009, Amy Carse guided in the Tetons, Wind Rivers, Cascades, Olympics, Wrangells, Smith Rock, Red Rocks, Joshua Tree, New Hampshire, France, Nepal, and Tibet. Amy opened new routes in Peru, including Artesonraju, Millishraju, Jatunriti, and Colquecruz, and made a first ascent of Dos Cuernos on the southern Patagonian Icecap in Argentina. Her numerous expeditions to the Himalayas include Muztagh Tower in Pakistan; the first ascent of Melanphulan in Nepal; and unclimbed peaks in Hongu, Nepal. She led the first unsupported American women's expedition to an 8,000-meter peak, Cho Oyu, in Tibet. Amy summited Everest in 2004 as a guide and climbing double for Universal Studios and guided Everest in 2007. She has climbed big walls in Yosemite and Zion National Parks; has guided for NOLS, Exum, Chicks with Picks, and Alpine Ascents; and served as program director of Khumbu Climbing School, Nepal.

Doug Coombs (Exum)

Doug Coombs, a two-time world extreme skiing champion, heli-ski guide, and pioneer of backcountry and steep adventure skiing, completed over 250 first ski descents in Alaska, Kyrgystan, Antarctica, Chile, France, Switzerland, and the United States. He earned UIAGM/AMGA certification as a ski mountaineering guide. His specialty was guiding steep adventurous terrain in the Chugach Range of Alaska and in the European Alps. Doug founded Steep Skiing Camps World-wide in 1993. Tragically, Doug died in a ski-mountaineering accident in 2006 near La Grave in the French Alps.

Nancy Feagin (Exum)

Nancy Feagin has made ascents of Mount Everest, Denali, and Aconcagua. She has made one-day ascents of El Capitan's Nose and Salathe routes, climbed 20 of Steck and Roper's *Fifty Classic Climbs of North America* in 20 days, and made an exploratory climb of Shipton's Arch, Xingjiang, China. Nancy has been featured in many climbing-related television and magazine advertisements, was a former film stunt double, and starred in the IMAX film *Extreme*. Nancy was the recipient of the American Alpine Club's coveted Underhill Award for climbing achievement in 2003.

Kent McBride (Exum)

Kent McBride has extensive guiding and instructing experience in all the realms of climbing and skiing. His work has taken him to many different areas around the world. Through utilizing his ability to organize exciting and interesting trips, pre-pare very challenging goals for his clients and helping them to hone their skills in the mountains, he has developed many lasting relationships. Kent is one of the few Americans who has passed the rock, alpine and ski mountaineering exams to become a UIAGM /IFMGA certified mountain guide. Over the past 20 years Kent has skied, climbed and guided in France, Italy, Switzerland, Spain, Argentina (Pata-gonia), Chile, Bolivia, Canada, Africa, Mexico, China, Tibet, Nepal, New Zealand, and major hot spots around the United States. He has also worked as a helicopter ski guide throughout Alaska, Greenland, and Chile. In 2005 he climbed to the central summit of Shishapangma (8,000 meters) in Tibet without oxygen and then completed the first ski descent of the Untsch couloir.

Mark Newcomb (Exum)

Mark Newcomb guided with Exum Mountain Guides for 19 years from 1990 through 2008. He also guided international adventure trips for Geographic Expe-ditions and helicopter ski trips for Valdez Heli-Ski Guides. His many expeditions include Denali's Cassin West Ridge and Cassin Ridge; a Shishapangma Unsch Cou-loir solo climb; an exploratory climb of Shipton's Arch, Xingjiang, China; a solo ascent of Chakragil; and a first ascent of Sepu Kangri. He made ski descents of Mount Vinson in Antarctica and the North Face of Shishapangma via the Unsch Couloir. Currently, he is an economic consultant and Teton County, Wyoming commissioner. Mark was a Watson Fellow in China. He earned an MS in Econom-ics and Finance from the University of Wyoming.

Al Read (Exum)

Al Read, a former president of Exum Mountain Guides, achieved first ascents in the Tetons and on the East Buttress of Denali. He was leader of first-ascent expeditions in Nepal of Gaurishankar and Cholatse, leader of the 1980 Minya Konka Expedition in China, and a member of the 1969 American Dhaulagiri Expedition (Nepal), and the 1986 Everest North Ridge Expedition. Al has been a U.S. Foreign Service officer and managing director of Asia's foremost mountaineering outfitter. From 1975–1984 he was vice chairman of Geographic Expeditions. He is a former board member of the American Mountain Guide Association. He was named to *Outside* Magazine's "A Team"—one of 25 "Best at Outdoor Adventure Professions"—in 2001.

Christian Santelices (Exum)

Christian Santelices believes that experiencing nature firsthand has the power to transform people's lives. As a fully certified IFMGA/UIAGM Mountain Guide, professional photographer, public speaker, writer, and community activist, his career has been dedicated to helping facilitate this process. Christian serves as a chief guide for Exum Mountain Guides, and also teaches avalanche courses, ski guides, and leads custom adventures and corporate community building and leadership development retreats worldwide through Aerial Boundaries. Christian dreams of creating a global community by engaging groups from around the world in common conservation efforts. To this end he established the Global Community Project (GCP), a nonprofit organization that combines outdoor education, service learning, and cultural exchange for students and professionals. The GCP provided the first sustainable trail building course to the rangers of Torres del Paine National Park, Chile.

Christian has made notable first ascents of big walls in Patagonia, including The Dream (VII 5.10 A4+) on the East Face of Cerro Escudo in Torres del Paine National Park, and numerous first ascents in the Sierra Nevada, California. With three friends he did the first (and only) ascent of 20 of Steck and Roper's *Fifty Classic Climbs of North America* in a single 20-day enchainment. As a guide, Santelices has led numerous expeditions to Patagonia; Aconcagua; Peru's Cordillera Blanca; the Alps of Switzerland, Italy and France; South Africa; the Pyrenees of Spain, the Atlas Mountains in Morocco; Fiji; Alaska; and Mexico. He has been featured skiing and climbing in numerous films, television programs, and print articles, including two Warren Miller films (*Journey* and *Impact*). Christian earned a BA in anthropology from the University of California at Berkeley, and an MA in environment and community from Antioch University, Seattle.

Jack Tackle (Exum)

Jack Tackle made the first ascents of Denali's Isis Face, Mount Hunter's Diamond Arête, Foraker's Viper Ridge, and Mount Barille's Cobra Pillar. Expeditions and ascents include peaks in the Canadian Coast Range and Mount Siguniang, China.

Other expeditions include Mount Everest West Expedition; Biafo Spires, Uzam Braak, and Biantha Braak (Ogre) in Pakistan; Cordilleras Blanca and Huayhuash in Peru; and Kashmir in India. He made the first ascents on Elevator Shaft, Mount Johnson, Alaska and Arctic Discipline on the North Face of Mount Kennedy in the Yukon. Jack's other first ascents include Mount Huntington, 2006; "The Imperfect Apparition" with Fabrizio Zangrilli; and the North Face of Mount Thunder, "Tangled up in Blue," and three new routes on the Mount Huntington massif, all with Jay Smith. Jack has served as a guide in the Tetons for Exum Mountain Guides since 1982 and is a former three-term director and treasurer of the American Alpine Club. He is the recipient of the American Alpine Club's coveted Underhill Award for climbing achievement (1999); the recipient of the Trento Film Festival and Italian Alpine Club award, "Genziana Giovanne" (1999); and the American Alpine Club's Sowles Award (2003). Jack is an AMGA-certified alpine guide.

Jack Turner (Exum)

Jack Turner's many accomplishments include pioneer climbing in Colorado, and extensive climbing in Yosemite and the Tetons. He is a veteran of 40 expeditions and treks in Pakistan, Peru, Nepal, China (Minya Konka Expedition), Tibet, and India. Jack is the author of the celebrated environmental works *The Abstract Wild*; *Teewinot, A Year in the Tetons*; and *Travels in the Greater Yellowstone*. Jack is an AMGA-certified alpine guide and a former president of Exum Mountain Guides.

Jim Williams (Exum)

Over the course of his career, Jim Williams has led major expeditions to Chile, Peru, Africa, Bhutan, China, India, Nepal, and Tibet. In 1989 he was the co-leader of the initial ski expedition to the South Pole, which was the first overland crossing to the South Pole from the South American side. Because of his familiarity with the extreme landscape and hazards of the Antarctic, he was selected as one of the leaders for the first commercial crossing of South Georgia Island along the route taken by Ernest Shackleton on his epic Endeavor expedition.

Jim has guided Mount Everest, Nupse, Lhotse, Denali, Ama Dablam, Carstensz Pyramid, Elbrus, and Aconcagua. His summit of Mount Everest in 2000 with clients inspired him to become the first person to successfully guide all "Seven Summits" (the highest point on each of the seven continents) in less than one year. Jim has been honored numerous times, and is the recipient of the National Park Service Search and Rescue Award, 2003. He was named a member in 2005 of the "Durable Dozen" in *Best Life* magazine for Seven Summits guiding achievement, and received the prestigious Explorers Club Lowell Thomas Award (2009) and the 2009 Exum Award for Excellence in the Art of Guiding. Jim is an AMGA Certified Alpine and Rock Guide.

Many other professional mountain guides and organizations were close partners in my research effort. Christian Santelices, founder of Aerial Boundaries Mountain Guides and co-chief guide for Exum, expertly guided several expeditions in the remote desert canyons of Utah, and others on high treks in Chilean Patagonia and Peru. Angela Hawse, an Exum guide and recipient of the 2011 Guide of the Year Award from AMGA, and Sue Muncaster also served as guides for Aerial Boundaries in Patagonia. Marco Palomino, founder of Culturas Peru, based in Cusco, and Zahan Billimoria, an Exum guide, served as co-guides with Aerial Boundaries in Peru. Arnar Már Ólafssson of Icelandic Mountain Guides introduced me to the wonders of Iceland, and Halldór Albertsson and his colleagues Herdis Sigurgrimsdóttir, Hrönn Jonsdóttir, and Katrin Petursdóttir guided us on many more extraordinary treks on Iceland's glaciers and snow peaks. Monica Pugh's outstanding staff at the Leadership Center of the University of Monterrey (UDEM), Mexico, welcomed us to their institution, put us through our paces on their stunning challenge course, and guided us in the local mountains. After participating in the National Outdoor Leadership School (NOLS) Pacific Northwest Trip Leader Program, I also visited NOLS headquarters in Lander, Wyoming, where John Gookin and John Kanengieter, among others, were very helpful and generous in sharing their views on expedition behavior and leadership. Each of these professionals has helped broaden and inform my view of the mountain guide as an exemplar of leadership, and I am grateful to them all.

About the Author

Chris Maxwell is a senior fellow of the Center for Leadership and Change Management at the Wharton School of the University of Pennsylvania. He previously served as adjunct professor of management and senior associate director in the McNulty Leadership Program at Wharton, where he organized and directed a wide variety of domestic and international outdoor leadership development programs in North America, Mexico, Patagonia, Peru, Quebec, and Iceland.

Chris holds two graduate degrees from the University of Pennsylvania (Master of Governmental Administration and Master of Applied Positive Psychology) and earned a PhD in public administration from Penn State. His work has been published in the *Wharton Leadership Digest, Wharton@Work, Organization Management Journal, The European Business Review, Journal of Surgical Education,* and the *American Journal of Public Health.*

Chris can be contacted through his website, www.leadlikeaguide.com.